Praise for *Let Him Lead*

"With this latest book, Fr. Jeremiah establishes himself even more firmly as a modern-day master of the interior life. Using everyday experiences and encounters, he weaves a rich tapestry of spiritual insight. These reflections, springing from a life of prayer and contemplation, are both accessible and inspiring, and are sure to benefit the reader who seeks closer union with God."

—Fr. Brian Graebe, STD, author of *Vessel of Honor: The Virgin Birth and the Ecclesiology of Vatican II*

"As a true preacher of the gospel, Fr. Jeremiah offers meditations that are at once easily accessible and challenging. Using familiar biblical stories, he asks, How is this aspect of the gospel becoming concrete in my life? Where is the Lord inviting me to a yet more complete response? As the gospel itself is "ever ancient, ever new," Fr. Jeremiah's meditations are applicable both to those just beginning to pray seriously and to every disciple wishing to be renewed and transformed through an encounter with the Lord in His Word."

—Mother Mary Concepta, S.V., Superior General of the Sisters of Life

"This book is a necessary reminder of the transformative power of the Gospels. If you long for an intimate relationship with Jesus, need a steady compass to guide you each day, or desire holiness but don't know where to begin, *Let Him Lead: An Invitation to Let Jesus Guide Your Heart and Your Life* is a must-read. Father Jeremiah's reflections offer a new perspective on familiar stories, inspiring us to seek more of Him when the world's promises don't deliver. If you buy one book this year, may *Let Him Lead* be the one–this is not a book to consume and forget, but one for a lifetime!"

—Laura Phelps, Content Creator at Walking With Purpose

"*Let Him Lead* stirred me to prayer. Fr. Jeremiah prophetically wants to set the world on fire through 'something greater than worldly wisdom.' His message is to follow the Lord, not fear, on a journey of love into eternity. A true son of St. Francis, he opens a contemplation of Christ in practical and breathtaking ways that draw from the Bible as well as the saints, great thinkers, and his own powerful personal stories."

—Dr. Anthony Lilles, STD, Professor at St. Patrick's Seminary and University and Co-Founder of the Avila Institute

"Simple, practical, and down-to-earth, Fr. Jeremiah offers a scriptural and compelling account of discipleship with the Lord Jesus."

—Fr. James Dominic Brent, OP, author of *The Father's House*

"*Let Him Lead* is a profound yet gentle invitation into the human heart. Father Jeremiah Shryock serves as a wise spiritual guide, leading the reader into a deeper understanding of universal experiences that we keenly feel, but may not always recognize, both on a natural and spiritual level. As he shares his own personal experiences, Father Jeremiah assures us that we are not alone—and that healing is within reach. Through insightful Gospel passages, Christ's living words, and the safety of God's unconditional love, *Let Him Lead* is a heartfelt invitation to greater spiritual freedom and deep intimacy in prayer."

—Megan Hjelmstad, Author of *Offer it Up: Discovering the Power and Purpose of Redemptive Suffering*

Let Him Lead

An Invitation to Let Jesus Guide Your Heart & Your Life

Jeremiah Myriam Shryock, CFR

PARACLETE PRESS
Brewster, Massachusetts

2025 First Printing

Let Him Lead: An Invitation to Let Jesus Guide Your Heart & Your Life

ISBN 979-8-89348-014-6

Library of Congress Control Number: 2025016733

10 9 8 7 6 5 4 3 2 1

Published by Paraclete Press
Brewster, Massachusetts
www.paracletepress.com

Printed in United States of America

Dedication

I could not have written this book without the presence of Mary, the mother of God, in my life. She is the way Jesus has first come to us in history, and she continues to be the way in which Jesus comes to me each moment.

Every day in prayer I ask Mary to be with me, pray with me, and reveal her son to me more deeply. In every homily I preach or talk that I give, in every spiritual direction appointment or apostolic endeavor I am involved in, I ask Mary to guide my thoughts, words, and actions so that they can reveal and glorify her Son. And as I sat down each day to write this book and reflected on the words of Jesus, I begged her to help me speak of him in a way that is true and beautiful, and most importantly, will lead people to want to seek Jesus more intensely in their own lives.

I simply could not have written this book were not the presence of this beautiful and Immaculate mother guiding me each day. Therefore, I give it back to her, since she knows Jesus best and since she was given to us by Jesus to be our mother in the order of grace (John 19:25–27). I ask her to do with this book what she deems best, knowing that everything she does is purely for the glory of God.

Contents

Foreword

Come, follow me! It is striking that Jesus uses these three simple words to call his first disciples. Jesus does not first propose a burdensome moral code, a political ideology, or some abstract idea to experience fulfillment and salvation. He first offers the gift of himself. Just think of the radical nature of what is happening here. In the fullness of time, Jesus comes to save all the sons and daughters of God by inviting them into a personal relationship with the living God. Jesus comes as Emmanuel, "God with us." He is the perfect revelation of the heart of the Father, bringing the fullness of love and mercy in his very person. When Jesus proclaims, *Come, follow me,* we are getting a glimpse into his Sacred Heart, a heart that aches for love and intimacy with you! It is this love that brings restoration and healing. All we have to do is *Let Him Lead.*

The experienced Christian knows that following Jesus is the joy of our life, but it also is the most demanding task we could ever take part in. In this broken and fallen world, we often experience our woundedness and limitations that have a ripple effect to all the different parts of our humanity. Sin and weakness blind us to the truth of who we are in Christ Jesus, and we suffer from an identity crisis. We no longer live as sons and daughters of the Father, but we live as orphans in a very strange world, seeking love and intimacy in places that do not satisfy. Brothers and sisters, you are not orphans! Jesus Christ, the Son of God, comes to restore and heal our identity so we can experience once again what it means to be sons and daughters of the Father.

In a very clear, engaging, and joyful way, Fr. Jeremiah is a witness and herald of these truths. Every chapter of this book is a sort of "icon" of the person of Jesus that invites you deeper into his Sacred Heart. Jesus came to earth because he does not want to remain abstract, but he longs to be known and loved by each one of us. In the Gospels, Jesus proclaims: "I am the way, the truth, and the life" (John 14:6)! Fr. Jeremiah fills these pages with the powerful truths that Jesus is the only *Way* to the Father and to true and lasting fulfillment. Jesus is the only *Truth* that is the source of our identity and destiny. Jesus himself is the *Life* that we long for, the fountain of love and intimacy.

Perhaps most importantly, Fr. Jeremiah reminds us of the "one thing necessary," which is love. Even in the Church, there is a strong temptation to make Jesus and the Gospels overly complicated, which keeps us focused on ourselves. Jesus reminds us that the key to life is actually letting go of ourselves and allowing one thing to remain: love. Jesus is the Son of God, and in his very person we encounter the perfect love of the Father. Living in this relationship of love and being an instrument of this love to others are the only things that matter. With power and light, Fr. Jeremiah bears witness to this truth. As a son of the Father, a disciple of Jesus, and a spiritual father, Fr. Jeremiah is a sure guide on our spiritual journey. All we have to do is *Let Him Lead.*

—Fr. Innocent Montgomery, CFR, author of *Born of Fire*

Introduction

In the Vatican II document entitled "*Decree on the life and ministry of priests,*" we are told that "*it is the first task of priests . . . to preach the Gospel of God to all men,*" and that "*their role is to teach not their own wisdom but the Word of God and to issue a pressing invitation to all men to conversion and to holiness.*"[1]

Every priest I know undertakes the task of preaching the gospel seriously. For some, preaching is a source of fear and anxiety, not because they are ashamed of the gospel, but because they are keenly aware of their own limitations. Other priests I know find preaching natural and a source of joy and consolation. Regardless of each priest's experience of preaching, the obligation to preach the gospel has been given to them. In a world that is becoming more and more secular, if the gospel is not preached, then where will people hear the Good News? Or, as St. Paul says, "*How are men to call upon him in whom they have not believed? And how are they to believe in him of whom they have never heard? And how are they to hear without a preacher?" (Romans 10:14).*

The question then for a priest is not *if* he should preach the gospel, for again as St. Paul says, "*If I preach the gospel, that gives me no ground for boasting. For necessity is laid upon me. Woe to me if I do not preach the gospel!" (1 Corinthians 9:16).* Rather, the question for all priests, and preachers of the gospel in general, is *how* they should preach the gospel. There are as many answers to that question as there are circumstances and situations in which each preacher finds himself. For example, on Easter Sunday the way I would preach about the Resurrection of Jesus if I were saying Mass in a prison would look and sound very different than if I were preaching in a country parish.

How I would preach about Easter would look and sound very different if I were preaching in a high school than if I were at a monastery. The difference is not the message, since *"Jesus Christ is the same yesterday and today and forever" (Hebrews 13:8)*, but how that message is articulated. A significant factor in determining how that message is articulated will be dependent upon who will be receiving that message, that is, the audience the preacher will be speaking to.

How does one proclaim the gospel to young people, the wealthy, the poor, those who are new converts, those who are spiritually mature, etc.? These are important questions every preacher must ask himself before he begins his primary task of preaching the gospel. The reason for this is obvious: we want to proclaim the truth of the gospel clearly so that each person, in their own uniqueness and varying circumstances, will be able to understand its message and respond to it.

When I wrote the reflections found in this book, I was living as a hermit at the Monastery of Bethlehem in Livingston Manor, New York, where I served the sisters there as their chaplain. While serving at the monastery I said Mass every morning for the sisters and those who were on retreat. Since the sisters live a life of solitude, prayer, and continual reflection on the word of God, I discerned that there was no reason for me to give a daily homily. After all, their monastic life was already nourishing their prayer life and their relationship with God. I did discern, however, to preach on Sunday, and so my primary audience for each Sunday homily was a group of 10–12 spiritually mature women whose life of prayer and meditation was well beyond that of a beginner.

However, there was a small minority of people who would also serve as my congregation for the Sunday homily: the retreatants. Each Sunday there would be anywhere from one to eight people who were on retreat and attending Mass and therefore would hear my homily as well. All the retreatants I met over the three years I lived at the monastery had a singular trait in common: They were all sincerely desiring holiness. After all, the decision to spend several days in solitude, silence, and prayer at a monastery completely removed from the comforts and pleasures of the world implies a certain level of seriousness and reflects a desire for holiness.

My little congregation on Sunday that I would preach to, then, was not a typical Catholic church in America, nor did it contain a specific group of people like those one would find at a prison, nursing home, or school. Rather, it was a diverse group of people of various ages and ethnicities who were all united in their chief desire to grow in a life of holiness. What then does that mean for a preacher? Primarily, it means that I could go a bit deeper. I could say things, challenge them in certain ways, or even provide a more advanced teaching regarding the life of prayer in a way that I couldn't if I were preaching at a high school or even a typical American parish.

Most people obviously do not live in a monastery, and unfortunately, many people are not able to go on retreat at one. Nonetheless, there are many Christians who sincerely desire intimacy and depth in their relationship with God. It is these people that I had in mind when several months ago I received the inspiration to take the outlines for some of my homilies and turn them into reflections for a book. The sole purpose for this is simple: to provide some means to help facilitate a greater response to Jesus in souls, or in other words, to inspire people to let Jesus lead them more deeply in their life by following him through the pages of the Gospel.

— 1 —

The World Is Never Enough

"Teacher, bid my brother divide the inheritance with me."
—Luke 12:13

The world's human population today consists of eight billion people. Among them are thousands of cultures and ethnicities, each providing a unique beauty to the richness of humanity. The seven continents on this planet comprise more than 57 million square miles of land, with wonders of nature that include enormous mountain ranges, tropical rain forests, deserts, and so much more. The five oceans that exist comprise 139 million square miles, most of which have not been explored yet, and contain 230,000 different species living in those oceans. This earth that we inhabit is truly a marvelous place.

Considering then the vastness and immensity of this world, one would think that this world would be enough for us, that here among so much beauty and diversity we could find what we are looking for and experience the peace that all of us so desperately desire. One would think that among all the remarkable features of life on this planet, the human heart could find rest and satisfaction. Yet humanity remains restless; people are continually searching not only in this world, but now, even beyond it. Why then does humanity keep searching in this world for its ultimate meaning and is seemingly never able to find one? Why is this world not enough for us? Many people have proposed various answers to these questions, but none provide an answer as fascinating as those found in the Bible. According to the Bible, the reason the world is never enough for us is, ironically, that it is too small.

In the book of Ecclesiastes, we read these famous words: *"Vanity of vanities! All is vanity" (Ecclesiastes 1:2)*. The book of Ecclesiastes is probably the least popular book in the entire Bible. I have heard many of my own brother priests lament this book when it appears in the lectionary either for Mass or in the Divine Office, because, according to them, the ramblings of Qoheleth, the author, appear to have no coherent theme or structure. I have heard some people admit that they cannot read this book because the author, they believe, is depressed, and they cannot understand or even tolerate his dark and negative outlook on life.

On the surface these complaints about the Book of Ecclesiastes can appear valid and sensible. However, if we listen more deeply to these words, the author is not intending to communicate to us a dark and negative view of human existence. Nor does he want us to believe that life in this world is miserable and that there is never anything to look forward to. Rather, he is telling us that life, just by itself, even amidst so much beauty and wonder, is not enough. It's not enough for the human heart, because the human heart can only find its completion and rest in the Infinite, in the One whose vastness and immensity knows no limits, and who has no beginning or end.

Several years ago, I was sitting in an airport awaiting a connecting flight when a middle-aged man approached me and asked if he could speak with me. I smiled at him, put away the book I was reading, and invited him to sit down next to me. Immediately he began telling me about his life. He was a travel writer who spent most of the year traveling all over the world and writing about his many experiences with all the people and places he was privileged to visit. Towards the end of our conversation, he looked at me with a tear in his eye and said to me, "Father, I have been almost everywhere in this world and seen almost everything, and I am not happy. I am always restless." A deep sadness filled my own heart when he said this as we both looked out the window of the airport. A few seconds later I asked him, "Have you ever thought about the One who created all this beauty and wonder that you are blessed to see." His response to me was shocking. He looked at me, both annoyed and frustrated, and said to me, "I just want this to be enough. I just want this world, my travels, and my career to be enough." I smiled at him and said as compassionately as I could, "This world is never enough, and it never will be."

In the parable of the rich fool (Luke 12:13–21) a man from the crowd approaches Jesus and says to him: *"Teacher, bid my brother divide the inheritance with me" (Luke 12:13)*. After Jesus refuses to heed this man's request, he then proceeds to tell the crowd a parable about a man who acquired a great deal of wealth and who decides that to store the surplus of his crops, he will tear down his barns to build larger ones. Once the larger barns are built and his crops are safely stored, the rich fool says to himself, *"You have ample goods laid up for many years; take your ease, eat, drink, be merry" (Luke 12:19)*. The world, it appears, seems to be enough for this man, and now he can sit back, relax, and enjoy life. However, this man's peace is short-lived, because as Jesus recounts in the parable, that night he will die. Jesus concludes the parable with a striking condemnation for those who not only believe, but also seek to find their peace in this world alone: *"The things you have prepared, whose will they be? So is he who lays up treasure for himself, and is not rich toward God" (Luke 12:20–21)*.

Are the things of this world important? Yes, they are, and Jesus never refutes that. However, they are not as important as eternity. To live only for this world or to hope that this world will be enough is to set oneself up for frustration and disappointment. Jesus is not denying or being insensitive to this man's earthly and material needs. However, he does not want him or us to simply remain here on this earth with only our earthly needs and desires. St. Paul, in writing to the Colossians, says, *"Seek the things that are above, where Christ is, seated at the right hand of God. Set your minds on things that are above, not on things that are on earth" (Colossians 3:1–2)*. It is only by looking beyond this world that we can live this life correctly, and this, according to Jesus, means being rich in the things of God.

How then practically do we live like this? First, we cannot ignore this world. As mentioned in the beginning, this world is truly a marvelous place. However, this world is not all there is. All the beauty and immensity of this world is meant to point to the immensity and beauty of God. The Psalmist understands this very well when he writes, "*When I look at your heavens, the work of your fingers, the moon and stars which you have established; what is man that you care for him?*" *(Psalm 8:3–4)*. To ignore this world then would be to ignore God. Second, we cannot ignore our life. All of us have material, physical and earthly needs that are simply a part of life in this world. However, we must not think that the purpose in life, or that our peace comes from the fulfillment of those needs. Rather, all these human needs, just like creation itself, are meant to be signs pointing us both beyond this world and even our own life. Whether it be in the beauty of creation or in the mystery of our own life, we can never stop and say, "This is it, this is what I've been looking for, this is what will fulfill me." Whatever "this" is can't be it, for the simple reason that it is too small.

There is nothing in this world then that can be pursued as an end. This includes our relationships, jobs, vocations, talents, friendships, and even our own life. So many of our frustrations and problems occur in life when we seek our fulfillment or end in the things of this world. I have witnessed so many friendships, marriages, and even vocations ending in heartache, anger, and deep emotional and psychological hurt, simply because either one person or several were hoping the other person would be someone they were not. In contrast to this, so much joy occurs and is available to us when we allow ourselves to be taken beyond this world to God, the true end for which we were created. A truly holy person witnesses to this joy in the depths of their being, because they are not attached or grasping at anything in this world. Rather, they are attached to and desire only God.

St. Basil writes, "*What, I ask, is more wonderful than the beauty of God? What is more pleasing and satisfying than God's mercy?*

. . . The radiance of the divine beauty is altogether beyond the power of words to describe."[2] The answer, of course, is *nothing*: Nothing is more beautiful and satisfying than God. May we truly live then in this world as pilgrims and follow both this world and our own life, in all its immensity and beauty, to the One who is even greater, to the One whose beauty and greatness knows no limits.

— 2 —

What Matters Most

"Even the dogs eat the crumbs that fall from their masters' table."
—Matthew 15:27

People often wonder where they are in their relationship with God. Over the years I have had countless souls ask me if there is some objective way or some practical tool they can use to measure their progress in the spiritual life or to determine where they are on the spiritual map. Numerous saints and theologians throughout history have suggested to us various means to answer these questions. In my own analysis and reflection, it appears to me that the answer to these concerns can be summed up in three questions: How pure is my faith? How confident is my hope? How selfless is my love? The honest answer to these questions will reveal to us where we are, really, in our relationship with God.

In the world today, both inside of Christianity and out, there is a great deal of hype about spirituality. People talk regularly in spiritual circles about things like consolations, methods of prayer, inspirations from God, one's own vocation and experiences of God in prayer, etc. Obviously, these are all very important and necessary for us, and each one of them is an essential component to our relationship with God. Nevertheless, by themselves, none of these aspects of the spiritual life make us holy, nor do they provide a valid measuring tool to determine the state of one's own soul. However, a person whose faith is becoming purer, whose hope is growing in confidence, and whose love is becoming more selfless—that person is becoming holy, regardless of whether those other things are present or not.

Now, there is both good news and bad news in this. The good news is that it is no secret what God desires of us. The genuine path to holiness, which will include light and darkness, clarity and confusion, and joy and sorrow, is ultimately the path of faith, hope, and love. St. John of the Cross affirms this when he writes, *"Faith and love"* (and we could certainly include hope) *"are like the blind persons' guides. They will lead you along a path unknown to you, to the place where God is hidden."*[3] This, then, is what the path of holiness looks like, and therefore this is how we are called to live.

The bad news about this is that usually—not always, but usually—the purity of our faith, the confidence of our hope, and the selflessness of our love are revealed to us, and grow most deeply, in darkness and in suffering. If God were to remove from a person the felt experience of his presence or a tangible experience of his grace, how much faith a person has at that moment is how much faith they really have. The same can be said about hope and love. It is easy to love God and another person when there is a tangible and felt experience of that love. Hence, when that love is reciprocal, not just in theory, but present amidst one's experience of life, it is easy to believe in the love of the other and to love in return. However, if you take away that experience, or if the other person appears distant or even not interested, how much love a person has at that moment is how much love they really have.

In the Gospel story of the Canaanite woman (Matthew 15:21–28), we are given a profound and beautiful illustration of all of this. This Gospel can be very confusing, and I will admit I spent many years puzzled by Jesus's actions and words in this passage, so much so that I would often not preach on this Gospel simply because I didn't understand what was occurring. A superficial reading of this passage can easily lead one to conclude that not only is Jesus being rude to this poor woman, but that he is not even interested in her.

St. Matthew recounts for us that a Canaanite woman comes to Jesus and cries out, *"Have mercy on me, O Lord, Son of David; my daughter is severely possessed by a demon" (Matthew 15:22).*

At first, Jesus does not even respond to her, and then we are told that *"His disciples came and begged him, saying, 'Send her away, for she is crying after us'" (Matthew 15:23)*. Finally, Jesus responds to her, but he tells her, *"I was sent only to the lost sheep of the house of Israel" (Matthew 15:24)*, implying that there is something wrong with her because she is a Gentile and not a Jew; therefore Jesus can't help her. Almost immediately then, there are three strikes against this poor woman.

It is worth stopping here for a moment and asking ourselves, how would we respond if we were this woman, and this was our experience of Jesus? Most likely, we would think to ourselves, *Where is the Jesus who opens the eyes of the blind and the ears of the deaf? Where is the Jesus who when Jairus comes and falls at his feet and says to him,* "My little daughter is at the point of death. Come and lay your hands on her, so that she may be well, and live" (Mark 5:23), *goes immediately to heal her? Where is the Jesus who says,* "Come to me, all who labor and are heavy laden, and I will give you rest" (Matthew 11:28)? If I were this woman, I would think to myself that either this Jesus whom I have heard so much about and whom everyone is talking about is either a fake, or he is simply not interested in me. Most likely, I would end up leaving him, disappointed, angry, and hurt. However, this woman responds very differently.

Rather than leaving Jesus she comes and kneels before him and begs him, *"Lord, help me" (Matthew 15:25)*. Once again, this woman makes herself totally vulnerable in front of everyone and in front of Jesus. Once again, she risks being ignored, considered a nuisance, and degraded. Once again, she will show the crowds, the disciples, and most importantly Jesus, that her faith is indeed mature, her hope is confident, and her love is selfless.

Every time I read this passage, I can't help but think that now Jesus will respond to her with love and gentleness, that now he will agree to go and heal her daughter. However, Jesus's response to her now appears even worse than before: *"It is not fair to take the children's bread and throw it to the dogs" (Matthew 15:26).* It is difficult to imagine a response more insulting than the one Jesus offers her, yet without hesitation she responds by saying, *"Yes, Lord, yet even the dogs eat the crumbs that fall from their masters' table" (Matthew 15:27).* This, I believe, is one of the most extraordinary responses, if not *the* most extraordinary response to Jesus from anyone in all the Gospels. The reason her response to Jesus is so extraordinary is because it is filled with a pure faith, a confident hope, and a selfless love. Even though she does not understand what is happening, why Jesus is saying these things, and where this is all going, her faith, hope, and love in Jesus remain intact. They are pure, confident, and selfless.

Why does Jesus respond to her in this way? I can't think of anyone else in the Gospel whom Jesus responds to like this after approaching him with such sincerity and humility. Jesus's response to her is meant to be a teaching moment, not for the Canaanite woman, but for the disciples and us. Through Jesus's words, though they certainly can appear harsh and insensitive, Jesus is teaching and attempting to show us that this woman is a model of discipleship. As the disciples watch this encounter take place, though they may be annoyed and irritated by her, they witness a woman standing before Jesus who will continue to pursue him, even if it seems that she is not being received in return. Hence, Jesus is attempting to show the disciples and us that if we truly want to be his disciples, then, like this woman, we must continue to pursue God even if it seems that he, and everyone else, are against us. We must continue to pursue God even when it might seem as if there is no hope or when it seems that God is absent, or that maybe he doesn't even love me.

By responding to this woman as he does, Jesus is drawing this woman deeper. Her experience of this moment in her humanity is one filled with darkness and suffering, because it can seem as if not only is she being rejected, but also she is even being ridiculed by him. Of course, Jesus is not rejecting or ridiculing her. Rather, by treating her this way he is attempting to elicit from her a deeper faith, hope, and love and to show us what authentic discipleship looks like. He can do this with her, and not with the disciples, because he knows the depth of her faith, hope, and love is great, and he wishes to call her even deeper.

If we wish to follow Jesus more deeply and grow in our relationship with him, then we too must strive for a purer faith, a more confident hope, and a more selfless love, because they are ultimately the only path that leads us to God.

— 3 —

The One Thing Necessary

"On these two commandments depend all the law and the prophets." —*Matthew 22:40*

As human beings we tend to think that life is difficult and complicated, perhaps because we have an uncanny ability to make life difficult and complicated. Anyone who has ever done even a minimal amount of soul searching or who is even vaguely familiar with the daily news is faced with the reality that life for most people is not something that comes easily. According to God, however, life is meant to be very simple, because life according to God comes down to one thing, and one thing only: love!

In the Gospel of Matthew, the Pharisees ask which, out of all 613 of the Mosaic laws, is the greatest. Jesus's response is simple: "*You shall love the Lord your God with all your heart, and with all your soul, and with all your mind. This is the great and first commandment. And a second is like it, You shall love your neighbor as yourself*" *(Matthew 22:37–39)*. For Jesus, life is very simple because the priority of all human life, and therefore the one thing that is truly necessary in life, is love.

If Jesus places such an emphasis on love, it is worth asking ourselves, why does God make love the priority of our lives? For those who are inclined to a more practical disposition towards life one could argue that Jesus makes love the greatest commandment because he wants all of us to get along, live in peace, and have order in our lives. After all, St. Paul encourages the Thessalonians "*to aspire to live quietly, to mind your own affairs . . . so that you may command the respect of outsiders, and be dependent on nobody" (1 Thessalonians 4:11–12).* As good as a quiet life and order are in one's own personal life and in society at large, the Incarnation has not taken place so that God can fulfill the role of a police officer whose sole purpose is to protect people from harm and keep order, as good and necessary as that role is. Rather, by commanding us to love, God is revealing to us ultimately the desire of his heart, which is that we, his creatures, become like him, because he, our creator, desires to share himself totally and completely with us. Because love is who God is and what God does, we become like God and share in his life only through love.

There are so many things in life that call out to us for attention and promise us fulfillment, peace, and satisfaction. Yet, no matter how good some of these things may be, or how attractive they might appear or even how wonderful they might make us feel, if love of God and love of neighbor are not in first place in our hearts, we will never truly be able to appreciate the things of this world appropriately, and therefore we will be constantly frustrated, disappointed, and restless. The simple reason for this is that our priorities are out of order. The things of this world, even though they may be good in and of themselves, are not meant to be the priority of our lives, which is why the only appropriate place for them is to remain at a distance from the love of God and our neighbor.

With all of this in mind, it would be helpful to sincerely ask ourselves, Am I loving God and my neighbor in my life right now? Or am I just simply thinking about loving God and others or pondering it during prayer? Love is one of those things that are easy and even consoling most of the time to meditate on and prayerfully consider. It is loving itself, though, not simply thinking or praying about it, that is the real challenge. If we desire to be authentic disciples of Christ and experience intimacy with God, saying yes to this challenge of love is never an option. Jesus reaffirms this when he says in the Gospel of John, *"By this all men will know that you are my disciples, if you have love for one another" (John 13:35).*

For each one of us to better assess the degree of love that may be present or absent in our life, I would like to propose a short examination for us regarding three areas of our life: prayer, relationships, and work. In my life of prayer am I truly loving God or am I just seeking to be consoled or entertained, or simply going through the motions? One of the dangers of having a relatively structured prayer life, meaning a certain time each day that I devote to prayer, is that my prayer can very easily become routine, and even though I may be there physically, my heart may be somewhere else. Hence, it is very possible, and even very probable at times, that during prayer I may not actually be loving God.

In my relationships or among those many different people that I encounter each day who qualify as my "neighbor," am I truly trying to love each person? Am I sincerely open to them? Do I treat the people in my life, whether I am naturally attracted to them or not, as means to a certain end? Am I consciously trying to love the neighbor in my life right now? It is often all too easy for us to discard certain people in our life, especially those many people whom we may not have a particular relationship with or those who are in some way estranged from family, friends, or society, as a nuisance or even a threat. By doing so not only do we fail to see the eternal significance for us of each person, but we also ignore Jesus himself, who in the Gospel of Matthew reminds us that it is he himself who is visiting us through others. Therefore, when we ignore them, we ignore Jesus, for, *"as you did it not to one of the least of these, you did it not to me" (Matthew 25:45).*

In my work, whatever form that may take, do I approach work with a loving and generous disposition, the disposition of a servant who freely gives of his time and talent for others? Or do I see work as simply something to endure, or something I do only for worldly gain or for a practical outcome? Or even worse, is my work merely an attempt to glorify my own ego so as to win the praise and esteem of others? The truth is, regardless of our occupation and the social class we may belong to, even the most basic and mundane job can have eternal consequences when that action is done out of love for God and others. Hence, the most important work, at least according to God, is not the one with the biggest paycheck, but the one that is done with the most love.

In one of his letters, St. John of the Cross writes, "*Where there is no love, put love, and you will draw out love.*"[4] Such simple, practical, and profound advice! Hence, if prayer has been difficult lately, dry, or even boring, choose to love God during prayer regardless of what your experience may be, and I guarantee your prayer will change—maybe not on an emotional and feeling level, but in the depths of your soul you will experience a shift. If there is tension or turmoil in a relationship, choose as best you can to love the other person regardless of what you may feel or what they might have done to you, and at the very least you will begin to change and most likely so will that relationship. If work is burdensome or difficult, try as best you can to offer your work for the love of God and others, and I guarantee you that your experience of work will take on a much deeper and even more fulfilling role in your life.

There is a fact about life that many of us, at the very least, find frustrating. The fact is that most of our life is out of our control. Despite our best wishes and sometimes even our best efforts, we cannot control God, the people in our life, or the circumstances and situations of our life. We cannot control our life because our life, at least exteriorly, is beyond us. However, what is in our control and not beyond us is how we respond to life. Jesus reminds us that the best response to life, the best way to live our lives, is make the love of God and neighbor our priority. Love, at least according to God as evidenced in his commandments, is the one thing necessary. It is the one thing that is always needed in our world, especially today, and it is the one thing that can simplify our lives and declutter our hearts and minds and help us to experience the simplicity of life that God always desires for us.

— 4 —
Hating Our Life

"If anyone comes to me and does not hate his own father and mother and wife and children and brothers and sisters, yes, and even his own life, he cannot be my disciple." —*Luke 14:26*

After St. Francis of Assisi experienced a deep conversion in his life, not only was he surprised by this newfound grace, but all the people of Assisi were surprised as well. As St. Francis would walk through his town, a town he was very familiar with, he would look around and see people he had known all his life busy about daily activities and seemingly oblivious to God. They, like most of us, were busy about what they considered their life. Seeing this caused St. Francis a great deal of sadness, not because people were busy working, but because they appeared unaware of God.

As he would walk through town, various people claimed to have heard St. Francis whispering to himself, *"Love is not loved."* He was referring of course to God, since *"God is love" (1 John 4:8)*. As he would walk by, mumbling this phrase, people began to think that St. Francis had lost his mind. Some felt pity for him since they knew his parents and had watched him grow up. *"What happened to this poor boy?"* many asked, while others ridiculed him and laughed at him, finding in St. Francis a buffoon in whom they could experience some entertainment and at the very least, a break from the humdrum of daily life.

What exactly did St. Francis mean by saying, *"Love is not loved?"* He was, I believe, lamenting over the spiritual state of the many townspeople he had known and loved his entire life. Ultimately, what St. Francis saw among his fellow townspeople was that their priorities were out of order, and because of this, their love was not disciplined. Hence, God, for the most part, was absent from their minds and hearts.

Jesus reminds us throughout the Gospels that he must be our first priority. For this to occur our love for everyone and everything else in life must be disciplined. Jesus expresses this truth in a very dramatic fashion when he tells us, *"If anyone comes to me and does not hate his own father and mother and wife and children and brothers and sisters, yes, and even his own life, he cannot be my disciple" (Luke 14:26)*. Upon hearing such an intense demand from Jesus, we must avoid two extremes when attempting to interpret such a statement.

First, we must not take these words literally and believe that Jesus is calling us to hate our family and our own life. Such an interpretation would contradict the fourth commandment, to love and honor our parents, and it would also contradict the inherent biblical precept that life is a gift (Genesis 1:31), and therefore is good. Second, we must not brush off this saying of Jesus as merely a poetic metaphor that he is using simply to get our attention. The truth, as usual, is somewhere in the middle. What then does Jesus mean when he tells us to "hate" our family and our own life? What practical consequence could this have for us in our daily life?

The word *hate* is defined as having an intense or passionate dislike for someone. However, when the word *hate* is used in the Bible, it means "to love less." In the book of Genesis, we read that *"When the Lord saw that Leah was hated,"* that is, loved less than Rachel, *"he opened her womb" (Genesis 29:31)*. Similarly, in the prophet Malachi we read, *"Yet I have loved Jacob, but I have hated Esau" (Malachi 1:3)*. Esau was "loved less," because he sold his birthright to his brother Jacob.

When Jesus tells us to hate our family and our life, he is telling us that nobody and nothing, even our own life and our own family, can be on an equal plane with God. Though this might sound extreme and even harsh, we are reminded of an important truth: All relationships and therefore all love, are not equal. We could call this the hierarchy of love. Imagine if a husband loved his friends in the exact measure in which he loves his wife, or if a teacher loved his students as much as his own children. All of us would agree that one's wife and one's own children should be loved more than one's friends or students. Why? Because the relationship that the husband and father possesses with his wife and children belongs to a higher category than that of friendship and students. At the pinnacle of this hierarchy of love is God, which is why Jesus will conclude in the Gospel of Matthew that *"He who loves father or mother more than me is not worthy of me; and he who loves son or daughter more than me is not worthy of me" (Matthew 10:37).*

Though most of us would agree with this teaching in theory, many of us find this teaching extremely difficult to put into practice. In listening to many people over the years as a priest, I have noticed that most of the struggles that occur in marriage, in religious life, and in friendships happen when we expect, demand, or even hope that another person takes the place of God. Despite our best intentions to *"worship the Lord your God and him only shall you serve" (Matthew 4:10)*, we create idols in other people, relationships, and life in general. When we live with this sort of hope and expectation, we are going to be endlessly frustrated. Our minds and hearts are never going to be at peace because our priorities are not ordered appropriately, and our love is not disciplined.

When I am preparing a couple for marriage, I always remind them that there is only one Savior, and your spouse is not it. They always tend to look a bit confused when I say this. However, a year or two after they have been married, they tell me that they now understand what I meant by saying that their spouse is not their savior. The same reality occurs in religious life. When a young man or woman enters a religious community, they tend to think that their community is perfect. At least I did. However, a few years later, and after they experience their own poverty and the poverty of all the members in that community more deeply, they begin to see that even their religious order is not their savior.

This can be very difficult for some to hear and accept. The primary reason, I believe, is because we live with the illusion that our life is actually ours. Without realizing it, this is the way we speak. We say things like, "my life, my vocation, my body, my time, my talents, my money," etc. Everything is mine, or so we think. Yet St. Paul offers us this sobering and thoughtful reminder when he asks the Corinthians, "*What have you that you did not receive? If then you received it, why do you boast as if it were not a gift?*" (*1 Corinthians 4:7*). The answer to St. Paul's first question quite simply is *nothing*, there is nothing that I have, even my own life, that I have not received from God. So then, why do I act as if it is mine?

St. Paul is alluding to a paradox that lies at the heart of the Gospel. If we really want to enjoy our life and to love our families and friends, then we must, to put it biblically, "love them less" than God and stop grasping at them in the hopes that they can satisfy us. It is only in this way that we can come to appreciate them most fully and love them in a way that is appropriate and meaningful. Without this mindset and disposition that the Gospel calls us to, we will always be forcing them to be someone or something they are not. It's not fair to them, ourselves, or God.

In the Gospel of Luke, the evangelist recounts that after a series of healings Jesus departs to a lonely place, while the crowds seek him out. Jesus could spend the rest of his earthly life in this one spot, healing, preaching, and drawing thousands of people to him. Despite the allure this may have for us, Jesus responds very differently. "*I must preach the good news of the kingdom of God to the other cities also; for I was sent for this purpose*" (*Luke 4:43*). Hence, despite the human affirmation, happiness, and even sense of fulfillment these crowds may bring to Jesus, there is something and someone greater than all of this: It is the Father and his will. Everyone else and everything else, Jesus "loves less," as he reaffirms when he tells us that *"my food is to do the will of him who sent me, and to accomplish his work"* (*John* 4:34).

Because Jesus loves everyone "less" than the Father—that is, he puts the Father first—those crowds that Jesus ministers to, including us, experience healing, forgiveness, and redemption. In a similar way, when we love everyone in our life "less" than God—that is, we put God first—others can experience the healing, forgiveness, and redemption of Jesus through our humanity because it is not grasping for attention and affirmation, nor is it attempting to manipulate life for one's own benefit.

The people of Assisi thought the young Francis was crazy because he went around saying, *"Love is not loved."* After his conversion, St. Francis realized that there is so much more to life than material gains, earthly satisfactions, and worldly popularity. It is not that these things are necessarily bad; however, what St. Francis realized is that none of these things deserve the fullness of our love, attention, and desire. This alone set St. Francis apart from many of his contemporaries, and quite honestly, even though he was looked upon as crazy, he was the sanest person in that town. He realized, thanks to the grace of God and the teaching of Jesus in the Gospel, that there is nothing and nobody in this world, as good as they are, and as beautiful as this life is, that compares to the goodness, beauty, and love of God.

— 5 —
Community as Healing

"Where two or three are gathered in my name, there am I in the midst of them." —Matthew 18:20

There is a beautiful story recounted in the lives of the Desert Fathers that highlights both the delicacy and attention that are required of us if we are to truly love one another. The story is as follows: One day three old men came to see the wise and holy Desert Father Abba Achilles. One of those men, it was reported, had a bad reputation. The first two men asked Abba Achilles if he would make them a fishing net so that they could have a souvenir of their meeting with this wise and holy Desert Father, and presumably show others. Abba Achilles responded by saying no to their request, because he said he did not have the time. The third man, the one with the bad reputation, stepped forward and asked Abba Achilles if he would make him a fishing net so that he could have something to take home with him to remember him by. Abba Achilles, much to the surprise of the first two men, responded to the man by saying yes.

Sometime later the first two men approached Abba Achilles and asked him why he said no to their request, but to the third man, the man with the bad reputation, he said yes. Abba Achilles answered:

> I told you I would not make one, and you were not disappointed, since you thought I had no time. But if I had not made one for him, he would have said, "The old man has heard about my sin, and that is why he does not want to make me anything," and so our relationship

> would have broken down. But now I have cheered his soul, so that he will not be overcome with grief.[5]

The reason that Abba Achilles said yes to making something for the third man had nothing to do with personal preference or monetary gain, or for the sake of receiving human praise and affirmation. Rather, Abba Achilles said yes to the third man because he knew that community life, whether it be in marriage, religious life, or in Christian friendships, is meant to be a place of healing and reconciliation, and not a place of division and conflict. Abba Achilles's decision to make a souvenir for the man with a bad reputation was not only an act of kindness, but also an attempt to facilitate healing in the soul of this man. By acting in this way Abba Achilles was simply following the teaching of Jesus.

In the Gospel of Matthew (Matthew 18:15–20), Jesus teaches us a three-step response to others who have sinned against us. First, we are to speak to the person alone. If he will not listen to us, we are to take one or two others with us. If that doesn't work, then we are to bring the matter to the Church. Jesus is not naïve in thinking that we will never experience division and conflict in our relationships with one another. Rather, Jesus is teaching us practically how to work through division and conflict. Why? Because he wants our life together as Christians to reflect the healing and reconciliation that he brings, since, as Jesus tells us in the Gospel, *"Where two or three are gathered in my name, there am I in the midst of them" (Matthew 18:20).*

Over the years I have become convinced, through my own experience both as a priest and as a spiritual director, that the number one tactic used by the devil towards faithful and devout people is to create division. I experience this temptation, not only within myself, but among everyone I encounter. It is prevalent in marriages and families, in religious orders and seminaries, and in ministry and friendships. In fact, I have noticed that often the main reason why a marriage, religious order, or ministry is not thriving has nothing to do with a lack of love for God, laziness, or inability, but rather it is because its members are divided. I have witnessed repeatedly throughout my life that once people are reconciled and united again their family or ministry begins to thrive again. Unity, even more than theological training or public speaking skills, seems to be, from God's perspective, the most important quality to strive for if we wish to grow in holiness and lead others to God.

Interestingly, the word "devil" comes from the Greek word *diabolos*, which can be translated as *"to divide," "to separate,"* or more literally *"to throw against."* It is the will of the devil to divide and separate us. Jesus himself experiences this in the three temptations he faces in the desert after fasting for 40 days and 40 nights *(Matthew 4:1–12)*. In each of the temptations that Jesus faces in the desert, the devil attempts to thwart God's word by tempting him to seek his own glory, thereby separating Jesus from the Father and destroying the unity they possess. The devil desires and loves disunity, whereas God desires and loves unity. Hence, it is the will of God to unite us, as Jesus prays in his high priestly prayer, *"that they (us) may all be one" (John 17:21)*.

Why is it the will of the devil to cause division? The answer is simple. Most likely, the devil knows that he will not be able to get faithful and devout people to reject the Incarnation, deny the real presence of Jesus in the Eucharist, or disregard any of the other major teachings of Christianity, but if he can create division among believers, he can limit their impact. By creating division, the devil can frustrate not only an individual's growth in holiness, but also that of all the other people who are in some way associated with that particular individual. When people are distracted by one another and turned in on themselves, their love for God and others is severely weakened. In short, their desire to live and proclaim the gospel is greatly compromised. What happens then? Nothing! Nothing happens, and that is exactly what the devil wants from believers: no growth in prayer, no practice of virtue, no forgiveness, no healing, and no reconciliation in our relationships. This is what division leads to—nothing—which is why it is so dangerous.

Why is it the will of God that Christians be united? Once again, the answer is quite simple. Our unity reflects the unity that is within the Trinity, within God himself. The Father, Son, and Holy Spirit are never divided among themselves. Rather, they are always and everywhere one. Therefore, our unity as Christians is ultimately a witness to God himself and a participation in his very life. Hence, unity is, in a very real way, "God-like," which is why reconciliation in our relationships is not merely a suggestion by Jesus, but is an essential component for our spiritual life, apostolic life, and our life in general with God.

Over the years, I have been asked by many sincere Christians how best they can grow in holiness. Understandably, many of them assume that they need to pray more, fast more, attend Mass more regularly, etc., and perhaps they do. However, after speaking with them about these areas I will always ask them, "How are your relationships? Do any of your relationships need healing and reconciliation?" These questions always appear to take people by surprise, and, almost always, they make them a bit uncomfortable. Generally, I have discovered that most people, including me, would rather talk about the spiritual life in general—things like prayer, spiritual reading, and retreats—than the state of their relationships. The reason for this is obvious: The state of our relationships is usually more troublesome and is often filled with wounds that a person would rather not look at or deal with.

The reason why I ask people about the state of their relationships is that if there are any relationships that need reconciliation, and there are always a few, this is just as important as prayer, fasting, spiritual reading, etc. In fact, if we prayed for several hours each day and fasted regularly each week, and never considered the state of our relationships, our progress in the spiritual life would be greatly limited and would eventually become stalled. Jesus emphasizes this in the Sermon on the Mount when he says, *"If you are offering your gift at the altar, and there remember that your brother has something against you, leave your gift there before the altar and go; first be reconciled to your brother, and then come and offer your gift"* (*Matthew 5:23–24*).

We would be foolish to believe that Jesus's teaching is easy and that it will not demand from us a great deal of effort. I, and I assume this is true for most people, would much rather spend an hour in prayer than have a difficult conversation with someone I'm struggling with or who has hurt me. I would much rather spend time reading a good spiritual book in some quiet place than ask forgiveness from another or accept forgiveness from another. However, we don't grow in holiness by only doing what we want or what is most comfortable for us. If we are serious about holiness then we must ask ourselves, Do we love the truth more than our ego? Do we love God's Word and what it asks of us more than our desires or what we find comfortable? If we do, then we must strive with all our effort to find reconciliation and healing in our relationships, not only because this is the will of God, but also because it is a great witness to the reconciliation and healing that are available only in God.

— 6 —

The Self I Must Deny

"If any man would come after me, let him deny himself and take up his cross and follow me." —Matthew 16:24

The essence of Christian discipleship can be summed up in the words of Jesus, *"If any man would come after me, let him deny himself and take up his cross and follow me" (Matthew 16:24).* These words can be easily misinterpreted as something that is negative, out of touch with reality, and even harmful to us physically and psychologically. The reason for such a dark view of Christianity is because some people assume that when Jesus tells us to "deny ourselves," then we must deny our very being and therefore forfeit the gift of life that God has given us. This can lead people to view Christianity as lifeless, joyless, and devoid of any human sentiments and experiences. Considering then the grave misunderstanding that can occur regarding Christianity, it is worth pondering for a moment, Who or what is this self that I must deny? Do I really have to deny my very own being and my own life? If so, why?

In the areas of both spirituality and psychology, there is quite a bit of literature about a "true self and a false self." Essentially, our true self is the self that has been made in the image and likeness of God (Genesis 1:26). Because original sin has greatly affected every aspect of the human person, we can find it difficult not only to experience but also to believe that we are indeed made in the image and likeness of God. Even though sin, both original sin and our own personal sin, has greatly distorted our human perception and understanding, in Christ and specifically through Baptism our relationship with God has been restored. Through the healing waters of Baptism our true self comes back into focus and thus enables us to perceive and understand once again who we truly are. St. Paul writes, "*We were buried therefore with him by baptism into death, so that as Christ was raised from the dead by the glory of the Father, we too might walk in newness of life*" *(Romans 6:4)*. Hence, through Jesus Christ those of us who have been baptized have become a "*new creation*" *(2 Corinthians 5:17)*, and enjoy, through no merit of our own, the status of a beloved son or daughter of God. Since that is true, St. Paul reminds us that our true life, and therefore our true self, "*is hidden with Christ in God*" *(Colossians 3:3)*.

It would be impossible to underestimate how revolutionary this way of thinking is and how contrary it is to the way of the world. For a Christian, one's true self, one's ultimate identity, has nothing to with career, social status, ethnicity, or the many other external things the world often associates as part of a person's identity, that is, their true self. Nor do we become our true self after building up a resume of accomplishments, whether they be worldly or spiritual, or by seeking them through the things of this world and gaining people's affirmation and attention. Rather, we become our true self simply by receiving it from God. Our true self then is the free gift of God's life and love to us, and we act out our true self when we are living as his children and when that is enough for us.

Our "false self," therefore, is someone entirely different. It is someone for whom being a child of God is not enough. Rather, the false self is that self within us that wants to be our own person, follow our own ideas and plans, make our own decisions, and create ourselves and our lives according to our own vision. Hence, the false self desires to live a life separate from God, and for all practical purposes the false self is choosing to be someone else other than who they really are. Regarding this false self, Thomas Merton writes, "*My false . . . self is the one who wants to exist outside of the reach of God's will and God's love—outside of reality and outside of life. And such a self cannot help but be an illusion.*"[6]

If the false self is someone who wants to exist outside of reality and outside of God's will, one may sincerely ask, who would really want to do that? The answer is, we all do to some extent! By simply looking at our daily life and examining some of our motives, actions, and words, we cannot help but admit that this is true. Sometimes we are conscious of this and sometimes we are not. Sometimes we deliberately plan to do so, while at other times it seems to happen almost naturally. Regardless, there are inside each one of us various motives, actions, and words that want not only to create this false self, but also to live from it.

Throughout the course of my priesthood, many people have asked me what I think the most important thing is that they can do in their spiritual life to grow in holiness. The obvious answer to this question is to live a sacramental life in a state of grace. However, as necessary as the sacraments and grace are to our relationship with God, simply receiving the sacraments is not a guarantee that one is growing in holiness. Because of this reality of the false self, the temptation towards illusion is prevalent inside each one of us. Therefore, the most fundamental and necessary work of the spiritual life is to spend time with God, or as Jesus says, "*Abide in me,*" since "*apart from me you can do nothing*" (*John 15:4–5*). We can spend time with God by meditating on his word, immersing ourselves in the liturgy of the Church, spending time each day listening to God and speaking to him in personal prayer, and trying as best we can to put his words and teachings into practice in our daily lives in the context of our own individual vocations.

When we are abiding in God our true self awakens from the slumber that our false self creates, and we become, over time, less inclined to be anyone other than who we really are in God. The reason for this is simple: The deeper our relationship with God, the more we encounter his utter goodness, love, and mercy, and the less tempted we are to desire a life separate from him. If we are not spending time each day with God the power and grace of the sacraments will be limited and have a minimal effect on us, not because there is something wrong with the sacraments, but because there is something wrong with us. What is wrong with us? We are not immersing ourselves in God and his life, and therefore we almost naturally slip into living for and fulfilling the desires and dreams of our false self, since that is who we know most deeply.

I once heard a priest friend of mine tell his congregation, "*The difference between a saint and a sinner is simple. A saint knows exactly who they are and who they are not, whereas a sinner has no idea who they are because they believe they are someone who they are not.*" To put it more simply, a saint knows that their true self can only be found in God. Therefore, they don't waste time looking for their identity among the things of this world. The sinner, unfortunately, believes that their true self is somewhere out there, among the passing things of this world, and they spend a great deal of time, sometimes an entire lifetime, looking for their true self where it cannot be found.

When we understand the complexities of our human nature, it is very clear that Jesus's words about "denying ourselves" are not negative at all but are in fact positive and even healthy. Nor are they out of touch from reality, but in fact they root us more deeply in reality because Jesus is attempting to spare us from the misery that follows from trying to live a life apart from him and from trying to have a "self" separate from God. In other words, he is reminding us that if we truly want to follow him, we must deny and even throw away this false self with this false life that it creates, and turn our entire self to him, who is truth and life, so we can discover who we truly are, but also who God really is.

People throughout history have attempted to create and live from this false self. When someone does this the result is always the same: a temporary happiness or a fleeting experience of fulfillment at best, yet when "*The rain fell, and the floods came, and the winds blew and beat against that house . . . great was the fall of it" (Matthew 7:27)*. The false self cannot withstand the many temptations, trials, and sufferings we face in this life simply because it has no foundation to stand on. Since the false self is built upon an illusion and a lie, its life expectancy is very short. Our true self, however, the self who really is in God, is the only solid foundation that can withstand anything and everything we may experience in this world. And that is because our true self is rooted in God, a foundation that cannot be destroyed, and whose life expectancy has no end.

— 7 —
A Love Story

"And the Word became flesh and dwelt among us, full of grace and truth; we have beheld his glory." —*John 1:14*

In the beginning of the Gospel of St. John, we are told that *"The Word became flesh and dwelt among us" (John 1:14)*. This one verse encapsulates the radical nature of Christian faith, namely that God has revealed himself to us completely in Jesus Christ. This revelation of God in Jesus Christ was not an astronomical phenomenon or something that occurred in nature amid great signs and wonders, but rather it took place in a specific culture, during a specific time, and in a specific way. In summary, St. John is telling us what no person could have ever imagined or predicted, nor what any religion or philosophy would ever dare to proclaim: God became man and lived among us. This revelation of God in Jesus Christ was not something abstract and distant from us. This theological fact is not merely a point of history but remains true for every disciple up to the present day. Every person who considers themselves a Christian can and should say that the revelation of God in Jesus Christ to them personally was not something abstract and distant from them, either. Rather, this revelation of God has occurred to them in their real life, through their own humanity, and amidst their own personal history. The implications of this for one's spiritual life are profound.

As a priest, I am often asked many questions on a variety of topics. However, the most consistent and common question I receive as a priest is this, *"Father, what am I supposed to do?"* The context for this question usually occurs when a person wants to speak with me about something they may be discerning or struggling with or even about how they can grow in their relationship with God. I am always a bit flattered and embarrassed that people would think that I, who wrestle with that same question in my own life, would be able to provide an answer to such an important and intimate question for them. However, rather than attempting to convince others that I have the answers to their life, I respond by first asking them a question: *"What happened to you?"* In other words, I am asking them, *"How did God reveal himself to you?"* Often this question leaves a person surprised and even annoyed, because it can appear that I am avoiding their question. However, the answer to my question is the key that unlocks the answers to many of our other questions regarding our life with God. By answering the question *"What happened to you?"* one can more easily discern things like, How should I pray? What is my vocation? Should I take this job or get involved in a specific ministry?, etc.

The question *"What happened to you"* is important for two reasons. First, it reminds us that the reason we are here, wherever that might be for us individually, is that "someone," not some*thing*, has revealed himself to us and has made himself known to us. St. John expresses this point most clearly in his first epistle when he writes, *"That . . . which we have heard . . . seen with our eyes . . . looked upon and touched with our hands . . . was made manifest, and we saw it and testify to it" (1 John 1:1–2)*. St. John is articulating a beautiful and important spiritual truth: Our life, faith, vocation, the desire to pray, etc., is the result of God making himself known to us. Hence, a Christian is not someone who needs to invent their life or discover clever ways to make their life fulfilling and meaningful. Rather, a Christian is one who receives their life totally from God. That life, the one that God has given us, is not lacking in anything. It is ultimately the life that our hearts long for and even need.

Second, that question reminds us that the entire Christian life is a response to the love of God, who has taken the initiative and first loved us and called us. Sometimes we can think we are so clever, that we are the ones who have figured out God or were seeking God first. Recently, I listened to a person recount their own conversion story, a story that was filled with much drama, excitement, and even miracles. However, while listening to this person I cringed at certain moments because they tended to talk more about themselves than God, implying that it was they who found God because they searched for him with a certain amount of passion, enthusiasm, and even intelligence. When they were finished speaking, this person asked me if I had any advice for them. I thought for a moment and replied very gently, *"Always remember that you did not find God, he found you, because you were not looking for him, but he was looking for you."* Then I quoted to him a passage from St. John's first epistle: *"In this is love, not that we have loved God, but that he loved us and sent his Son to be the expiation for our sins" (1 John 4:10).*

What then can we conclude from all of this? The Incarnation, God's revelation to us collectively and individually, is a reminder that the Christian life is ultimately a love story. God, the ultimate lover, the desire of every human heart, has revealed himself to us for the simple reason that he loves us and wants us to love him in return. The Christian life, whether you are a monk, nun, married, or single, is a witness to this "someone," namely Jesus, entering our lives and transforming us from the inside out. What is the specific means of transformation that God uses to change us? It is himself in the person of Jesus Christ through whom we are changed.

The question *What happened to you?* thus becomes the key that unlocks the answer to many of our questions regarding our life with God. So many people ask, "What should I do with my life? How should I pray? Should I enter this vocation?", etc. The answer to all those questions is, *Where is Jesus?* Wherever he is, follow! If Jesus has made himself known to you in the poor, go to the poor. If Jesus has made himself known to you in solitude, go into solitude. If Jesus has made himself known to you through preaching, go preach! Wherever Jesus is, follow him.

Towards the end of his life St. Francis wrote a short work that is called *The Testament*. In this work St. Francis is essentially recounting God's grace in his life and how God revealed himself to him. In the *Testament* St. Francis says that "*When I was in sin, it seemed too bitter for me to see lepers. And the Lord himself led me among them and I showed mercy to them. And when I left them, what had seemed bitter to me was turned into sweetness of soul and body.*"[7] Though these words may not appear deeply profound, these three sentences sum up what was the essence of St. Francis's story, namely that he encountered Christ in the poor, specifically in the lepers, which took him by surprise and drastically altered his life.

Francis's encounter with Jesus in the lepers is going to play as the background music for the rest of his life. This is why St. Francis can't become a monk or a hermit because the Lord led him to the lepers. Monks and hermits generally do not work with the poor because it's not their charism, nor is it often the way the Lord has revealed himself to them. Franciscan life, this new way of living the gospel, began because St. Francis responded to the way in which God revealed himself to him.

So, what about you? What is the essence of your story? *What happened to you?* The way that God revealed himself to you is your own personal and unique love song. There is nobody else in the world who shares the same song that God has sung to you to get your attention. This song is completely your own, because God has written and sung it to you in a way that is so personal that if someone else were to hear it, they would be unable to recognize it. God doesn't reuse conversion calls, moments of grace, or awakening experiences. Every single one of them is unique to each person. If we want to become holy, authentic, and the person God made us to be, then we must keep this song close to our hearts and make sure it is not drowned out by the songs of others.

One of the greatest temptations that all of us face in life is comparison. If we are married, we can quite often compare ourselves to other married couples. If we have been given the ministry of preaching, then very often we compare ourselves to other preachers, and so on. Though this may be a normal human experience, if we don't guard against it, it can be very harmful for us spiritually. Every time we compare, we are almost always led to despair. Comparison distracts us from the grace of God that is present in our life right now and turns God's presence into absence. It is not uncommon that when a person is comparing themselves to others they will ask God, "*Where are you?*" I have asked God that question repeatedly throughout my life, and every time he answers in a similar way: "*I was with you until you decided my grace for you was not enough and you started comparing yourself to others. If you want to experience me again, come back to where I am for you.*"

Imagine if St. Francis listened to St. Benedict's song or if St. Teresa of Calcutta listened to St. Clare's song. We wouldn't have a St. Francis or a St. Teresa. Furthermore, if you and I do not become saints, it is most likely because we did not hear our own song. God forbid that should ever happen to any of us! Yes, we must imitate the saints in their love, abandonment, and gift of self to God; however, none of our lives are identical to theirs. To become the saint that God desires us to be, we must hear and follow the unique song that God sings to us today.

— 8 —
The One Thing Certain in Life

"Not a hair of your head will perish."
—Luke 21:18

Imagine that you have been planning a vacation for months. You have worked hard to be able to afford all the expenses and have even made certain sacrifices in your own personal and social life for the sake of being able to take this vacation. You wake up on the first day of your vacation, and for the first time in months, you are genuinely excited about life and bubbling with happiness. You arrive early at the airport, go through security and are now waiting patiently at the gate to board your plane. Once your row has been called to board, you jump up from your seat and rush to the front of the line. As you board your plane, you smile at the flight attendants, stow your luggage in the overhead compartment, and introduce yourself to the person sitting next to you. While the flight attendants close the door to the plane and make a final check of the passengers before takeoff, you look out the window and breathe a deep sigh of relief and say quietly, *"Thank you, God."*

After a few moments, the pilot comes over the intercom and introduces himself and his crew and tells the passengers that the flight they are about to embark on will experience a tremendous amount of turbulence. Because of this turbulence they will have to wear their seatbelt for the entire flight, and they will not be able to move around. Also, he says that they will be flying through several storms on their flight and the plane will, most likely, get struck by lightning. Because of this, the flight attendants will not be able to serve them on this flight. There will be no food or beverages available, which is probably good, since they will not be able to get up and use the restroom. The pilot then reassures all the passengers on board not to worry, because he says, he knows how to fly under such conditions.

Everyone on board begins to look at each other in horror and disbelief. *"Is he serious?"* many ask. *"This can't be happening."* Some jump up from their seats and demand to exit the plane, while others frantically try to call the flight attendants for help or scroll desperately through their phones seeking other travel options. Suddenly, your calm and peaceful vacation that you have been waiting for has taken an unexpected turn for the worse. You are now left anxious and afraid and begin questioning whether taking this vacation was the right decision. What do you do? Do you stay on the plane? Or do you consider other options?

Most likely, we have never heard such an announcement in our life. Thank God! However, what this story attempts to illustrate in a dramatic fashion, is a fact about life that most of us would rather not admit. The only thing certain about life is that it is uncertain. No matter how much we plan, prepare, and even pray, none of us can be assured that life will follow exactly as we expect or even hope. The truth is it rarely if ever does. And why should it? Neither life nor God promises to fulfill our plans, ideas, and goals. Yet we often feel offended, slighted, annoyed, and frustrated when life doesn't work out the way we expect. We think that life, and even God, owes us something, and that our life, instead of being a gift given to us by God, is a right we deserve or have even earned, and one that God should reward us for in earthly measures. If this is our attitude about life then obviously we will be continually frustrated, for we will be searching for certainty in the one place it most assuredly is not, namely in our own life.

In the Gospel of Luke, Jesus makes an announcement to the disciples that is even more dramatic than the one the pilot made in the opening story. He tells them, *"Nation will rise against nation . . . there will be great earthquakes, and in various places famines and pestilences (Luke 21:10–11).* As if that were not enough to scare us Jesus continues, "*They will lay their hands on you and persecute you, delivering you up to the synagogues and prisons. . . . You will be delivered up even by parents and brothers and kinsmen and friends, and some of you they will put to death; you will be hated by all for my name's sake (Luke 21:12, 16–17).* Jesus concludes his announcement by assuring us, "*Not a hair of your head will perish*" *(Luke 21:18).*

Hidden amid all the apocalyptic images and themes, in this Gospel passage Jesus is intending to teach us where true consolation and hope can be found, which is in the fact that there is nothing more certain than God. Specifically, there is nothing more certain than God's presence, as Jesus himself affirms when he tells us, "*I, when I am lifted up from the earth, will draw all men to myself*" *(John 12:32).* There is nothing more certain than God's love, since "*God so loved the world that he gave his only-begotten Son, that whoever believes in him should not perish but have eternal life*" *(John 3:16).* Finally, there is nothing more certain than God's care for us, as Jesus reminds us when he says, "*If God so clothes the grass of the field, which today is alive and tomorrow is thrown into the oven, will he not much more clothe you, O you of little faith?*" *(Matthew 6:30).* Jesus is reminding us that even when everything else may seem and feel as if it is falling apart, even amidst the turbulence, the lightning strikes, and the rude passengers, God is certain. Therefore, Jesus says at the end of his "announcement," "*Not a hair on your head will perish*" *(Luke 21:18).* Why? Because he is with us.

Several years ago, I was a preaching a retreat to a community of Poor Clare nuns. The superior asked me on the first morning of the retreat if I would be willing to spend an hour or two speaking with their novice director.

"Of course," I told her. "Should I meet her in the chapel this afternoon after my talk?" I asked.

"No, Father," the superior said. "She is in the hospital. I can drive you there after your conference."

The novice director, I would discover, was a deeply beloved sister in the monastery who at the age of 53 was diagnosed with terminal cancer, and at the time I was there preaching the retreat, was only given six months to live. On my way to the hospital the superior was telling me how desperately they were all praying for a miracle and how saddened the entire community was because of what appeared to be her imminent death. Despite their tremendous faith and their extraordinary prayer life, this nun's sudden sickness had shaken their entire community, not only because they loved her so dearly, but because it was a reminder to them of the uncertainty of life, even their life with God.

When I approached her room at the hospital I knocked and heard a faint but calm voice telling me to come in. Even though I had never met this nun before in my life, as soon as I entered she smiled at me as if I was an old friend whom she hadn't seen in years. She was holding a rosary in one hand and a small crucifix in the other and told me to come and sit down next to her. For the next hour or so we talked about everything from her childhood, her vocation, to her suffering with terminal cancer. She shared with me how much she loved being the novice director, because, as she said, working with the young women who had just entered the monastery helped to rekindle awe and wonder at her own vocation. When I asked her what the most difficult part was about being in the hospital, she said it was being separated from her sisters and having to pray alone all day. Despite these sufferings, being in very serious physical pain, and living with the awareness that her days on this earth were limited, she radiated a peace and joy that I have rarely seen in anyone.

At one point in our conversation, she looked up at me with a smile on her face and said, "Father, nothing in my life turned out the way I planned or expected." She paused for a moment and then continued, "And for that I am so grateful, because it turned me away from myself and towards God." I was shocked by her words. Usually what I hear from others, and what I have said at times, is something like this:

"My life has not turned out the way I planned or expected. Why has God allowed this? Why has God abandoned me? Because of this I am miserable." Instead of searching for God in the way our life really is, and being grateful for the way our life has unfolded, most of us become sad, annoyed, and deeply troubled when we realize that our life has turned out very differently from what we either planned or hoped.

After I talked with her for a few more minutes, it was time for me to return to the monastery to give the next conference to her sisters. I smiled at her, blessed her, assured her of my prayers, and thanked her for her witness of faith and began walking towards the door to leave. As I opened the door to leave, her faint but calm voice cried out, "Father."

"Yes, sister," I said and turned towards her.

"God is certain, do not be afraid of anything," she said. Then she quoted the beautiful words of St. Teresa of Avila that she not only had memorized but had clearly interiorized as well: *"Let nothing disturb you, let nothing frighten you, all things are passing away: God never changes. Patience obtains all things. Whoever has God lacks nothing; God alone suffices."*[8]

All throughout the Gospels, Jesus affirms the uncertainty of life, whether in the parable of the rich fool (Luke 12:13–21), or in Jesus's teaching regarding where our true treasure must be (Matthew 6:19–21), or the parable of the talents (Matthew 25:14–30), or in so many other instances. The conclusion found in all these passages is a sobering one. Jesus never promises us peace in this life. In fact, He tells us, *"Do not think that I have come to bring peace on earth" (Matthew 10:34)*. Therefore, we can guarantee that things such as wars, natural disasters, and scandals in the Church and in the government will remain, and that sickness and even pandemics will continue throughout history. It also implies that humanity's great efforts to thwart some of this uncertainty, which is good and necessary, are limited, and that humanity despite all its intelligence and good will, will never be able to erase uncertainty from life as a whole and from our own individual lives.

Therefore, how do we respond and live in a world filled with uncertainty? We must turn our hearts more deeply, not away from the world and all its uncertainties, but more intensely towards God, the one and only thing that is certain. When our faith, hope, and love are centered completely in God, our lives and our hearts will be, as Jesus says, *"built . . . upon the rock" (Matthew 7:24)*. In other words, we will not be as shaken and terrified when we experience turbulence, storms, and difficult people in life. This does not mean that we will never struggle in life or that we will understand perfectly everything that is happening in the world and to us. Something greater than worldly wisdom is being offered to us, namely, the grace to see through this world to its ultimate source, which is God. A God who seemingly keeps trying to tell us throughout our entire life, *"Don't worry, I know how to take care of you under such conditions."*

No matter how much turbulence we may face in life, God is guiding the plane, and he always brings us home.

— 9 —

Can I Trust God?

"Man shall not live by bread alone,
but by every word that proceeds from the mouth of God."
—Matthew 4:4

All of life comes down to one basic question: Can I trust God? If I cannot, then my life will become a frantic attempt to protect myself and try to ensure both an identity and a life that corresponds with my own vision and desires. If I can trust God, then my life will become, not an active pursuit of my own ideas and desires, but a gentle surrender to the presence of God, found most often amid the circumstances and situations of daily life. Whether those events are joyful or sorrowful, beautiful or difficult, the person who is attempting to trust God more deeply sees not only the circumstances and situations of his own life, but also the mysterious presence of God in those moments.

I often encounter people who tell me they have difficulty believing in God because of the state of the world or because of the tragedies and trauma they have experienced in their own lives. I am always sympathetic to such people, because I can understand how from a rational point of view, life with all its pain and suffering can cause one to doubt both the existence of God and the goodness of God. Of course, I do not believe that pain and suffering disprove the existence of God, but rather I can understand how one could struggle with trusting God, especially if one has suffered greatly in this life.

Many years ago, I was at a gas station when a 30-year-old man approached me and asked if I could talk with him for a few moments. I finished pumping gas and parked my car and spoke with this man on the sidewalk for about 30 minutes. Several months back, he told me, his wife and five-year-old daughter had been killed in a car accident by a drunk driver. Understandably, he was still suffering greatly and asked, if there was a God, how could he allow this tragedy to occur?

I simply sat there on the sidewalk and listened to him voice his anger and frustration at life, God, and even me as a priest, all of which I understood and was not offended by at all. However, at the end of our conversation, the last words that he said to me with tears in his eyes were, "I guess I need to trust God." I smiled at him and said, "Me too."

In the Gospel of Matthew we read that immediately after Jesus was baptized, he was led into the desert *"to be tempted by the devil" (Matthew 4:1)*. The evangelist records that after Jesus fasted for 40 days and nights the devil appeared to him to tempt him. At the heart of each temptation, the devil was attempting to make Jesus stray from the Father's will, proclaim his independence from the Father, and ultimately take control of his own life and destiny. In short, the devil was seeking to undermine God the Father's credibility, that is, his trustworthiness. However, when Jesus was confronted by the devil in the desert, there was not a moment of hesitation or doubt that occurred within him. Unlike Adam and Eve (Genesis 3:2), Jesus did not enter into dialogue with the devil, but rather responded immediately with the Word of God: *"Man shall not live by bread alone, but by every word that proceeds from the mouth of God. . . . You shall not tempt the Lord your God. . . . You shall worship the Lord your God and him only shall you serve" (Matthew 4:4, 7, 10)*.

What is Jesus saying to the devil by responding to him purely with the Word of God? In the desert, as at the crucifixion, Jesus's disposition is the same, *"Father, into your hands I commit my spirit" (Luke 23:46)*. Jesus is proclaiming to the devil that his trust is in the Father, and that God the Father is trustworthy. This is why many of the Church Fathers saw in the temptations of Jesus an "Adam typology"[9] occurring, meaning that just as Adam is cast out of paradise into the desert because of his infidelity and lack of trust, Jesus, who is the new

Adam, goes into the desert to rescue us by his fidelity, which is marked primarily by his trust in the Father.

Jesus's response to the devil in the desert is a reminder for us of two facts. First, without trust in God, our life will easily be swayed by every temptation, every suffering, and every tragedy we experience in life. Every time we experience difficulty or confusion regarding the mystery of life, without trust in God we will be tempted to seek refuge in ourselves. We will be tempted to believe that we are alone in this world, that we must provide everything for our lives, and that we cannot trust anyone, especially God. This attitude is a recipe, not only for misery, but also for a life of constant tension, anxiety, and fear.

Second, Jesus's response to the devil in the desert also highlights where we can find the answer to the question "Can I trust God?" The answer to that question, strangely enough, can be found in the desert, where God's trustworthiness is revealed to us in such a profound way. Often, life can feel like a desert, especially when we are experiencing loneliness, boredom, rejection, or so many other human experiences that can leave our hearts and minds feeling dry and even abandoned.

The desert, at least biblically, is a place where a significant amount of interior activity is occurring. It is a place of temptation, purification, and combat, but ultimately, the desert is a place of formation. What was God attempting to do with Israel in the desert for 40 years? He was trying to teach her to trust him. He was trying to show Israel that he was guiding her, that he loved her, and that he was providing everything she needed. As God himself said to Israel, "*You have seen what I did to the Egyptians, and how I bore you on eagles' wings and brought you to myself*" *(Exodus 19:4)*.

Jesus's own example of going into the desert echoes this same reality. He is trying to teach us to trust him. He is trying to show us that he is guiding us, that he loves us, and that he is providing everything we need. "*When I sent you out with no purse or bag or sandals, did you lack anything?*" Jesus asks his disciples later in the Gospel. Their response? "*Nothing*" *(Luke 22:35)*. The conclusion is simple. When we allow ourselves to trust God, even amidst the difficulties of this life, we will experience, in a very mysterious way, God's drawing us to himself, where, as we will discover, we lack nothing.

Many centuries ago, the prophet Jeremiah wrote,

> Blessed is the man who trusts in the LORD. . . .
> He is like a tree planted by water,
> that sends out its roots by the stream,
> and does not fear when heat comes,
> for its leaves remain green,
> and is not anxious in the year of drought,
> for it does not cease to bear fruit.
> (Jeremiah 17:7–8)

There are many people today who would dismiss these words and label them as old-fashioned religious piety, not applicable to sophisticated modern people. Yet there are other people, who, upon hearing these words, desire that they may be true, but struggle to believe, and therefore live, as if they are.

Even though these words can be difficult to believe and therefore live, and even though they were written in a different culture, in a different time, amidst a vastly different experience of life, these words of the prophet Jeremiah are filled with both wisdom and sanity, even for us modern people. The truth is that life both changes and doesn't change. Yes, things like technology, science, and medicine have all greatly enhanced human life, all of which we are grateful for. However, none of these gifts to humanity have been able to provide the existential reasoning or cause for human life. Only God, ultimately, is the reason for and the cause of all human life. Therefore, if our life is to have any real meaning and depth to it, it must be lived consciously with him.

Yet, living life with God, as we all know from experience, is not always easy. He does not text us or email us or communicate with us in the way we are used to in the modern world. His presence and how he communicates with us are more subtle, since after all, he is God and not a human being. Spiritual activities like prayer, reading Scripture, and receiving the sacraments are excellent means of strengthening our relationship with God and enabling us to hear his voice more deeply. However, how do we live a deeply spiritual life when life seems confusing or even depressing? How do we live a deeply spiritual life when prayer and Scripture appear dry or even boring? How do we live a deeply spiritual life when we are suffering, whether physically, psychologically, or emotionally?

The only answer is trust, trust in God. All the saints, prophets, and mystics throughout the centuries have both taught and showed us in their own lives that trust in God is our only security and the only sane way to live this life. If we look at our lives prayerfully, even those moments where we experienced suffering, darkness, and confusion, did we lack anything? In other words, even in our suffering, were we not given, in some mysterious way, the grace to move through that suffering? If not, then how could we have ever made it through those moments and be where we are today? The truth is, without God, we could never be where we are today. Without God, there is no today. Therefore, the only way to live our lives is by trusting in God, since after all, he has proved himself trustworthy.

10
A Spiritual Examination

"Who do you say that I am?" —*Matthew 16:15*

In the Gospel of Matthew, Jesus proposes a question that we are all very familiar with, a question that we may have spent many hours praying with and pondering: *Who do you say that I am?* We cannot exaggerate the importance of both this question and our answer to it, because this question is by far the most important question we will ever be asked in life. How we answer this question will reveal who we really believe Jesus is, and not only does our answer to this question have implications for us in this life, but also its effects will follow us into eternity.

The Church's answer to Jesus's question, its theological foundation, is based upon Peter's answer in today's Gospel: The *Catechism of the Catholic Church* teaches, "*Moved by the grace of the Holy Spirit and drawn by the Father, we believe in Jesus and confess: 'You are the Christ, the Son of the living God.' On the rock of this faith confessed by St. Peter, Christ built his Church*" (CCC 424). Therefore, the Church's answer to Jesus's question is not a secret. She confesses, believes, and proclaims that Jesus of Nazareth, born of Mary in Bethlehem, who suffered, died, and rose from the dead is the long-awaited Messiah, the Savior of humanity, who is God.

The theological nature of this question, then, has been settled, and every follower of Jesus accepts this truth and believes it. However, the distance from one's head to one's heart is often the longest journey to undertake in this life. The mere belief in something, or in the case of

Christianity, someone, does not automatically imply that one's behavior, attitude, and mindset have been or will be transformed. In other words, consenting to a particular belief will not guarantee a tangible and practical change in our day-to-day lives. For this transformation to occur, there is often much struggle, temptation, and suffering that we must face, not to mention discouragement, doubt, and desolation as we experience our own inner poverty and weakness. Most of us can relate to St. Paul, who once confessed, *"I do not understand my own actions. For I do not do what I want, but I do the very thing I hate" (Romans 7:15)*. Regardless of the difficulties that the journey from one's head to one's heart entails, this is ultimately the pilgrimage that each one of us must make if we desire to follow Christ more deeply.

With all this in mind, I would like to use Jesus's question *Who do you say that I am?* as a means for us to examine our own life of discipleship. How am I living as a disciple of Jesus? Is my faith in Jesus merely an intellectual idea? Or is it something that affects my whole being and my entire life? In what areas in my life is the presence of Jesus lacking? The reason for this examination is simple: The Incarnation is not merely an idea, nor is it simply an event in history. Rather, through the Incarnation, the ultimate purpose of human life is revealed to us in a most stunning way. We are called to become *"divinized,"* or as St. Peter expresses it, to *"become partakers of the divine nature" (2 Peter 1:4)*. Hence, through the Incarnation we are invited to share in the very life of God, that is, to become God-like. For this to occur in us, every part of us—our hearts, minds, and souls—must be transformed so that our thoughts, words, and actions reveal the glory and love of Jesus, the one who we hold is God.

To help facilitate this examination I would like to focus on three specific areas of our life as disciples: prayer, community, and suffering. These three areas, I believe, are the most prominent areas of our life as disciples because they are the ones we experience most readily.

Regarding our life of prayer, let us examine the question "*Who do you say that I am?*" If I really believe that Jesus is Lord, that "*the Word became flesh and dwelt among us" (John 1:14)*, do I, specifically in prayer, reveal myself to Jesus? Do I share with him my pain, my joys, my hopes, my fears, and my weaknesses? Is prayer something I look forward to and make time for each day? Is my prayer personal, honest, and sincere? Am I really trying to look at Jesus, to listen to him, and to open my heart to him? Am I trying to love him in prayer and grow in love? Am I open in prayer to receive Jesus and his revelation? Do I persevere in prayer when it may be dry, dark, or even boring? Do I read books and seek the counsel of others so that I can grow in my prayer life? Do I beg the Holy Spirit to teach me how to pray?

Or is prayer for me simply a mechanical repetition of words, actions, and sentiments that have no flesh or heart to them? Is prayer something I do to merely check off my "to do" list so I can move forward to what's really important in life and to what is more practical? Do I use prayer as a time to simply think about myself and consider how I can improve myself, and appear stronger, smarter, or even holier than others? Do I consider extra work and times of service as a substitute for solitary prayer, therefore excusing myself from time alone with God because I am doing things for God? Do I fill prayer time with reading, devotions, or other things that prevent me from listening and simply being with God in prayer?

Regarding our life in community—and this could be life in a religious community, in a family, or in the Church community to which one belongs—*"Who do you say that I am?"* If I really believe that Jesus is Lord, do I strive to see his presence and hear him in others, especially in those whom I find difficult, those towards whom I might not have a natural affinity or attraction? Am I trying to forgive those who have hurt me in life, whether intentionally or unintentionally? Do I make myself available to serve those around me? Am I attentive to the needs of those around me? Do I really listen to others when they speak to me? Am I open to strangers, the poor, or those who are in need, whether they are in my community, family, or neighborhood? Am I trying to be patient and compassionate towards those who might not be as quick, intelligent, or competent as I am? Do I take seriously Jesus's own words when he says, *"By this all men will know that you are my disciples, if you have love for one another" (John 13:35)?*

Or am I simply closed in on myself, always thinking about myself, and what I need, what I want, and what I desire? Do I allow fear or laziness to prevent me from giving myself to others in generous service? Am I distracted by the things of the world and the flesh that prevent me from even seeing opportunities for love and service to others? Am I so concerned with protecting and building up what I consider to be "my life" that I have no time for others? Am I afraid to reach out and serve others because of past hurts, disappointments, or even traumas?

Regarding our experience of suffering, which is something we all have experienced and will continue to experience in the future: *"Who do you say that I am?"* If I really believe that Jesus is Lord, how do I respond, or how am I living right now with suffering, whether that suffering is physical, emotional, psychological, or even spiritual? Do I suffer with Jesus, meaning, do I offer him my suffering and see it as a means to unite myself more deeply with him? Does my suffering increase my faith, hope, and love in Jesus? Do I allow the purification that suffering brings to humble me and increase my desire for Jesus the Divine Physician? Do I remind others, and even myself, that suffering is not a punishment from God, but can be a means to a greater union with him? Am I patient in times of suffering, trusting in God's love and mercy? Am I quick to reject feelings of desolation, doubt, and even despair when I am experiencing suffering?

Or when I am suffering do I spend most of the time complaining, feeling sorry for myself, and blaming others? Do I seek unhealthy ways to numb the pain that suffering can cause? Does suffering make me doubt God or even question his goodness? Or am I bitter and angry at God for the suffering that either I or someone I love has experienced? Do I run from suffering and try to hide from it to the detriment of my own health, whether it be physical or psychological?

As we can see, Jesus's question *Who do you say that I am?* affects our entire life as disciples. This question is not merely a theological one reserved for scholars and theologians to debate. Of course, Jesus's question has theological implications, but the beauty and grandeur of this question far exceeds the confines of a particular discipline, even one as important as theology. Jesus's question encompasses the entire gamut of human existence. Therefore, every person, if they wish to take their life seriously, must prayerfully consider this question and come to a conclusion.

However, let us not be fooled. We cannot merely ponder and answer Jesus's question only once in our life or only in times of prayer and retreat. If we really want to take the gospel seriously and live it in its entirety, then we must ask ourselves this question every day of our lives and allow it to form us, so that our thoughts, words, and actions, and even the desires of our hearts, can match not what we believe in, but WHOM we believe in.

11
Fear Is a Liar

"Take heart, it is I; have no fear." —*Matthew 14:27*

In the beginning of my senior year in college, after many years of discernment, I made the decision that, after graduation, I would join the Franciscan friars of the Renewal in New York City. Whereas most of my peers spent their senior year anxiously writing resumes, searching for jobs, and preparing for their future careers, I spent most of my senior year, when I was not in class, quietly praying in a nearby chapel or going for long walks in the country. Hence, my senior year in college was relatively peaceful, as I was filled with both wonder and excitement about what my future as a Franciscan would be like.

About a month before I was scheduled to leave home and move to New York City to join the Franciscans, I woke up one morning with a paralyzing fear. The fear, like most fears in general, was completely irrational. It made no sense, and I have no idea where it came from. It had nothing to do with religious life, living the vows of poverty, chastity, and obedience, or leaving my family and friends. Nonetheless it was there, weighing heavily on my heart, and sending my mind into a panic. The fear was that if I moved to New York City, I would never be able to drive again. The reason I would never be able to drive again was that everybody in New York City drives like a crazy person, or so this fear was telling me. Therefore, there were only two options. Either I join the Franciscans and just tell them I can't drive, which really wasn't an option, or I drive and most likely die in a car accident.

Despite this incessant fear that had taken hold of me shortly before I entered the Franciscans, I moved to New York City on September 8, 2002. On September 10, the moment I had dreaded for the last month became a reality. After class that afternoon in the Bronx, my postulant director looked at me, handed me the keys to our minivan and said to me with a huge grin on his face, "Why don't you drive home?" Not seeing a way out of this situation, I took the keys, got into the van, and waited for my other classmates to arrive. A few minutes later I pulled out into the streets of New York City and thought to myself, "Well, this is it. I had a good life. Thank you, Jesus." However, 15 minutes later something miraculous occurred: I pulled up to the friary in Harlem, and everyone, include me, was still alive.

That evening during Eucharistic adoration I remember looking at Jesus in the host and reflecting on what had just occurred a few hours prior. I realized that this intense fear that I had regarding driving in New York City was for the most part untrue. In fact, it was a lie. I began to consider how much time and energy I had wasted entertaining this fear and this lie. I began to wonder, if this was true about this fear, what about all the other many fears I have had in life. Were they all a lie as well?

In my own opinion, and after much experience with this, I believe that after sin, fear is the greatest obstacle in our relationship with God. The simple reason for this is that fear ultimately paralyzes us. What happens when we are paralyzed? It becomes difficult, if not impossible, to move. However, that is not all. Fear also makes us hesitant, not only towards ourselves and others, but most importantly, towards God. When we are hesitating towards God, we begin to doubt God's love, his goodness, and his ability to provide everything that we truly need. When this attitude creeps into our heart, the purity and intensity of our faith, hope, and love will be greatly reduced, because we are turned in on ourselves. In other words, how I respond to God and how I receive his love will be greatly compromised because of my fear.

In the Gospel of Matthew, Jesus tells the disciples to get into a boat and meet him on the other side of the sea while he goes up into the hills to pray. After some time has passed, a storm develops, and the disciples become understandably afraid. As the waves are beating against their boat, Jesus leaves the hills and walks on the water out to the disciples. However, the disciples are unable to recognize Jesus. Their fear has clouded their vision; therefore, they are not able to see things clearly, and they believe Jesus is a ghost. Jesus immediately attempts to calm their fear by telling them, *"Take heart, it is I; have no fear" (Matthew 14:27).*

Peter, filled with both sincerity and zeal, calls out to Jesus and says to him, *"Lord, if it is you, bid me come to you on the water" (Matthew 14:28).* After Jesus tells Peter to come, Peter begins to walk on the water towards Jesus. However, Peter very quickly becomes afraid, because he takes his eyes off Jesus and begins to focus on how strong the wind is. As Peter begins to sink, he cries out to Jesus to save him, and immediately Jesus reaches out his hand, catches him, and says to him, *"O you of little faith, why did you doubt?" (Matthew 14:31).* Why did Peter doubt? Because he was afraid, and fear clouded his vision and closed his heart. Hence, his relationship with Jesus suffered greatly because of his fear.

It is worth asking ourselves why the disciples are afraid in this Gospel passage. The disciples are afraid for the same reason we are: The challenges in life—in the disciples' situation a storm at sea—appear beyond their ability to control. When we are not in control we tend to panic, because we realize we are not strong enough, competent enough, and holy enough to deal with life in all its complexities and challenges. The disciples and we are absolutely right for thinking this because we are none of those things. However, what Jesus is attempting to teach them and us is that he is all those things. He is strong, holy, and wise, and he loves us more than we will ever be able to comprehend. Hence, in the presence of Jesus, fear is exposed to be what it really is, a lie!

After reading this a person may think, "Yes, fear is a lie—there is nothing I need to be afraid of." Though that is true, the next time this person experiences fear, which could be a few minutes after this realization, they may assume that because they are experiencing fear, their faith is weak. We must distinguish between simply feeling fear, whether in our body or our psyche, and living in fear. When a person is living in fear, many if not all of their decisions, thoughts, and actions are controlled and dominated by fear.

It is unrealistic to think that faith in Jesus will prevent us from ever experiencing fear in this life. Even Jesus in his humanity experienced fear during his agony in the garden. St. Luke recounts that during Jesus's prayer in the garden of Gethsemane that Jesus *"prayed more earnestly; and his sweat became like great drops of blood falling down upon the ground" (Luke 22:44)*. However, he did not allow himself to be controlled by fear. *"Not my will, but yours, be done" (Luke 22:42)*, Jesus prayed to the Father.

The goal then that all of us should be striving for and praying for is the ability to not be enslaved by or controlled by fear and to not allow it to influence our decisions, our treatment of others, and our response to the grace of God in our lives. Furthermore, maturity in faith enables us to not believe—at least as much as we may have before—what fear is trying to tell us.

Each one of us has encountered and will continue to encounter many storms in life. However, the presence of Jesus is ultimately our remedy against fear, because his presence alone conquers all things. Sometimes God will remove things in our life that cause us fear. If that occurs, we must praise him and thank him for it. However, most of the time he does not, because he wants to do something better than remove from our life that which is causing us fear.

This transformation is impossible if, like Peter in the Gospel, we have taken our eyes off Jesus. The next time we are experiencing fear, good questions to ask ourselves are, "Where is my gaze right now? Am I looking at myself, others, or Jesus?" It is safe to say that most if not all our interior sufferings occur when we have taken our eyes off Jesus and are either focused too much on ourselves, other people, or the things of this world.

How then can I respond to fear in my relationship with God? This question, and the answer that proceeds from it, are essential not only for our human maturation but for our spiritual growth as well. The answer is twofold. First, we must pray for the grace not to simply overcome our fears or even ask God to remove our fears, but to walk through our fears with Jesus. Second, we must, as much as possible, consciously choose to walk through those fears practically each day, but again, with Jesus.

For example, imagine that a person is afraid of applying for a job, devoting more time to prayer, or having a difficult conversation with someone. Our priority when we experience fear in these or any other situations is first to express honestly and humbly to Jesus in prayer our experience of fear, and then to beg him to accompany us through this fear. However, we must remember that most people, most of the time, do not hear voices or have visions when they pray. Therefore, if after praying and expressing our fears to Jesus we don't hear or see anything, we must not assume that God is not listening or is not interested in us. Rather, we must believe that God hears us, loves us, and is providing us with the grace that is necessary to walk through this fear.

After praying and speaking to Jesus about our fears, the next thing for us to do is to walk straight towards them, or if that seems like too much, at least not try to avoid them or walk around them. Practically speaking, if I'm worried about having a difficult conversation with someone, I cannot be deliberately trying to avoid meeting such a person so that the conversation will never happen. The irony here is that the more I avoid fear, the greater it becomes, whereas when I confront fear, it loses both its magnitude and power. The biblical wisdom for this approach can be found in the words of Jesus to St. Paul, *"My grace is sufficient for you" (2 Corinthians 12:9)*. Hence, God is already giving us all that we need in life. It is up to us to not only believe this, but to act upon it.

Throughout my life, I have encountered, and I still encounter many fears, whether it be driving in New York City, speaking in front of thousands of people, or even writing a book. Regardless of the number of fears I have experienced, each one of them has revealed this one fact to me, namely that fear is a lie. Do not think that I am a particularly strong or courageous person for saying this, because I am not. I have simply learned this answer from being in the presence of Jesus.

12

The Authority of Jesus

"They were astonished at his teaching, for he taught them as one who had authority, and not as the scribes."
—Mark 1:22

When I was growing up, I had a wide assortment of friends. For the most part, my friends were not athletes, honor roll students, or the typical kid next door. Rather, they were artists, musicians, and deep thinkers. We were not concerned about popular opinion or political correctness, but truth. Each one of us in our own way was seeking the ultimate meaning to life and what our purpose in this world was. Nonetheless, all my friends were very intelligent, creative, and passionate about life, but, unfortunately, not very religious.

When I began to experience a reversion to Catholicism in my late teens and started discerning a vocation to religious life, they were shocked, surprised, and mostly confused. As sincere as all my friends were, and despite how hard they tried to understand what was going on with me, they simply could not. Regardless of all their best efforts, my friends reduced everything that was happening to me through their own ideals and human categories. For example, some of my friends believed that by returning to Catholicism and entering religious life, I was adopting Catholicism as a philosophical ideal. For them, Catholicism was a system of thought that I found appealing and convicting. Others, because I would be entering the Franciscans and working with the poor, concluded that I was dedicating my life to social justice and spending my whole life attempting to ease the plight of the poor. Some of my other friends, the more politically radical ones, believed that my vocation was a rebellion against American middle-class society and therefore a rejection of the values and ideals that capitalism instilled in the masses.

As idealistic and even noble as some of those explanations might have been, none of them were true. My friends were interpreting reality through the only means they knew—their own ideals and human categories. They did this because they didn't know Jesus. My return to Catholicism and my religious vocation did not find its source and inspiration from anything in this world. It came, quite literally, from beyond it.

At the core of every conversion and vocation is an encounter with the presence of Jesus, and his power and authority. Christianity is not a philosophy, nor a system of morality, nor a branch of social justice. It is first and foremost an encounter with Christ, with his power and authority, which is meant to dramatically change the life of the one who encounters him. Pope Benedict XVI articulated this in a beautiful way in his first encyclical entitled "*God is love.*" He wrote: "*Being Christian is not the result of an ethical choice or a lofty idea, but the encounter with an event, a person, (Jesus Christ) which gives life a new horizon and a decisive direction.*"[10]

The Gospel of Mark records an episode where Jesus enters a synagogue and begins to teach. The people in the synagogue are "*astonished at his teaching . . . [and] were all amazed" (Mark 1:22, 27)*. Why? Because "*he taught them as one who had authority, and not as the scribes" (Mark 1:22)*. During his teaching, a man with an unclean spirit approaches Jesus and begins to call out to him. Unlike the exorcists of Jesus's day who would have to recite long prayers and exert tremendous effort to expel demons, and unlike the scribes and Pharisees who would ultimately be helpless before an evil spirit, Jesus simply commands the spirits, "*Be silent, and come out of him!" (Mark 1:25)*, and they obey. The evil spirits are unable to resist the power and authority of Jesus, which is why at Jesus's command they are *"convulsing . . . and crying with a loud voice" (Mark 1:26)*.

The power of Jesus's presence is a witness to his authority and a sign of his divinity. Jesus has authority, unlike the scribes, because he is God and he is demonstrating to everyone in the synagogue his divinity by his authority. This is why the demons cannot withstand his presence. This is why, as we see throughout the Gospels, Jesus has power over nature (Mark 4:39), over illness (Luke 4:39), over death (John 11:43), and over sin (Mark 2:5). There is simply nowhere in the Gospels where Jesus is presenting himself as a philosopher, social worker, moralist, or even simply another religious figure in the long history of world religions. This is also why conversion and vocation cannot be reduced to merely human ideals and categories, even good ones like morality, social justice, or philosophy.

The word *authority* appears 38 times in the New Testament, and it almost always refers to "divine power," or "the power of God." Hence, authority in the Bible is not a reference to human strength or a political victory, but the strength and power of God. Jesus references this "divine power" repeatedly. *"That you may know that the Son of Man has authority on earth to forgive sins" (Matthew 9:6). "Neither will I tell you by what authority I do these things" (Matthew 21:27). "All authority in heaven and on earth has been given to me" (Matthew 28:18)*. When Jesus speaks and acts, unlike the scribes and the Pharisees, and unlike anyone else in human history, he is speaking and acting as God, because only he has this authority.

A common opinion among many today is that Jesus Christ is only a religious figure, just like Buddha, Mohammed, or the Old Testament Prophets. Jesus's presence and his teaching, this opinion maintains, is not unique and therefore does not require any special adherence to it.

He is simply one teacher among a long line of "awakened" souls, and his teaching, especially the Beatitudes and his teachings on forgiveness, though often considered noble and praiseworthy, are simply the musings and visions of a holy man. They are not considered the words of God.

The problem with this thinking is that it not only contradicts the authority of Jesus's actions, but it also contradicts what Jesus says about himself. What prophet or holy person says things like, *"I am the bread of life; he who comes to me shall not hunger, and he who believes in me shall never thirst" (John 6:35). "I am the resurrection and the life; he who believes in me, though he die, yet shall he live" (John 11:25). "I am the way, and the truth, and the life" (John 14:6).* Prophets, holy persons, or awakened souls do not speak like this. If they are authentic, they always point away from themselves to someone or something greater, whereas Jesus is pointing to himself. In these verses and in so many others in the Gospels, the uniqueness of Christianity is being revealed, namely that God has come to us and has revealed himself totally and completely in Jesus Christ.

However, even if we do believe that Jesus is God, surrendering to his authority for many people is not easy. The word *authority* makes many modern people nervous and almost instinctively rebellious, simply because there have been so many bad examples and abuses of authority throughout human history. I am constantly amazed by the stories people share with me regarding abuse they have experienced, whether it be emotional, physical, psychological, or even spiritual, from those who have had authority over them in life. This abuse can come from parents, spouses, teachers, employers, and unfortunately, even those in the Church. When a person has experienced abuse in any form, and regardless of what degree of abuse occurred, a person will naturally, and understandably, find it difficult to surrender to the authority of Jesus.

However, we must consider the nature of Jesus's authority and how he desires to use it in our lives. Even though certain human beings have used their authority to control, manipulate, and repress others, Jesus uses his authority as God not as a weapon against us, but as a remedy for our own healing and salvation. In other words, Jesus's authority is a healing balm for our souls, and therefore surrendering more deeply to it is the path that all of us must choose to walk if we wish to experience the fullness of liberation and transformation that the Gospel proposes.

In the Gospel of Luke, as Jesus is about to begin his public ministry, he enters the synagogue, opens a scroll, and reads from the prophet Isaiah. The passage that he reads is Isaiah 61:1–2, a passage loaded with Messianic undertones and expectations. In this passage, the prophet Isaiah declares that the Messiah has been *"anointed . . . to preach good news to the poor . . . proclaim release to the captives and recovering of sight to the blind, to set at liberty those who are oppressed" (Luke 4:18–19)*. Once Jesus finishes reading this passage he sits down and says to the crowds, *"Today this Scripture has been fulfilled in your hearing" (Luke 4:21)*. Not only is Jesus telling the people that he is the Messiah, but he is also telling them how he will use the authority that is his, namely for our healing and redemption.

Unfortunately, I have lost contact with many of my old friends. However, occasionally I will speak with a few of them on the phone, and every few years some of us will meet at a diner for lunch and catch up. Many of them are still seeking truth; however, philosophy, art, and music have not provided them with any clarity and meaning to their lives, but have in many ways only given them more questions and have caused a greater amount of restlessness inside them.

The last time I was meeting with them, my childhood friend Philip pulled me aside and said to me, *"I'm still surprised and shocked that you are a Franciscan priest."* We both laughed, and I responded by saying, *"So am I!"* Then he got a very serious look on his face and said to me in a whisper, "*Like you, I am starting to become fascinated by Jesus, spirituality, and prayer.*" I sat and talked with him for a while in his car, and as I was leaving, I said a prayer with him and promised to pray for him each day.

Like many people in the modern world, Philip is fascinated by Jesus, spirituality, and prayer. This is good, but it is not enough. A disciple of Christ, someone who accepts Jesus's authority and therefore believes he is God, must be fascinated only by Jesus. If we are fascinated by Jesus, our prayer life, spiritual life, and understanding of who Jesus is and our experience of him will grow in ways we could never imagine. The reason for this can be summed up in Jesus's own words, "*If you continue in my word, you are truly my disciples, and you will know the truth, and the truth will make you free*" (*John 8:31–32*). If we truly wish to be free, then we must surrender ourselves more deeply to the authority of Christ, since only through his authority can we find the peace, healing, and redemption we all need.

13
Love Is a Journey, Not an Experience

"The wise took flasks of oil with their lamps."
—Matthew 25:4

About a month ago I received a phone call just after I finished celebrating Mass. When I looked to see who was calling, my whole body became tense, and I started to panic. I immediately assumed the worst. It was my 23-year-old nephew. The reason I began to worry is that my nephew, like most young people, prefers to text me rather than speak on the phone. If I had to guess, I would conclude that my nephew has only called me once or twice in his whole life, and both times it was to deliver bad news. This time would be no exception. I answered the call immediately and asked what was wrong. He told me he had just broken up with his girlfriend.

I closed my eyes and breathed a sigh of relief, saying to myself, "*Thank God!*" I was grateful, not because I didn't like his girlfriend or that I was happy their relationship was over, but because nothing more serious had occurred. I took a moment to tone down my relief so I could listen to him and be compassionate and available to offer any counsel that he was willing to receive. I asked him what had happened, and he told me that he couldn't see himself being with her in the future, couldn't see himself marrying her, so there was no point for them to stay together.

I was both shocked and edified by his words. Without realizing it, my nephew was articulating a truth about authentic love that appears to have almost been forgotten in a culture addicted to instant gratification. So often, people evaluate their relationships with others or even with God based on the emotional or spiritual highs they have experienced. The truth that my nephew was articulating is this: Authentic love is revealed not so much in an immediate experience or feeling of another, but in the decision and willingness to journey together with the other. To the extent that we are willing to journey together with another, whether that other is God, a spouse, a friend, or someone we work with, the degree of our love or lack of love for that person will be revealed.

If a person is simply seeking an experience or an emotional high with another, they will never find love. Why? Because they are essentially seeking themselves through the other and are using the other for their own self-satisfaction. However, those who are willing to journey together with another will, almost always, both find and experience authentic love, because they have placed the other person and not themselves at the center of the relationship.

All of this is expressed more deeply in the Parable of the Wise and the foolish Maidens (Matthew 25:1–13). In this parable, Jesus compares the Kingdom of heaven to ten maidens who take their lamps to meet the bridegroom. Five of these maidens are foolish and five are wise. The five foolish maidens do not bring enough oil for their lamps, while the five wise maidens are adequately prepared. Finally, after a delay a cry is uttered: *"Behold, the bridegroom! Come out to meet him" (Matthew 25:6)*. As all the maidens prepare to meet the bridegroom, the five foolish maidens do not have enough oil for their lamps. They beg the five wise maidens for some of their oil. However, the wise maidens refuse, because in giving some of their oil to the foolish maidens there might not be enough for them also. The five foolish maidens then must leave the place where the bridegroom is to buy oil for their lamps. While they are away, the bridegroom arrives and takes the five wise maidens in with him to the marriage feast and shuts the door. Finally, once the foolish maidens have purchased oil for their lamps and returned, they knock on the door to the marriage feast, saying, *"Lord, lord, open to us" (Matthew 25:11)*. The bridegroom responds with these harrowing words, *"Truly, I say to you, I do not know you" (Matthew 25:12)*.

Why are the five foolish maidens called foolish? On a practical and literal level, they were foolish because they did not bring enough oil for their lamps, something that anyone with minimal experience and intelligence would do. However, a deeper reading of this parable reveals that the main reason they were foolish is that they did not realize that love is a journey and not an immediate experience. Hence, they were unprepared both interiorly and exteriorly for a deep and intimate relationship with the bridegroom, because they were seeking a quick and immediate experience of him. Hence, they were not sufficiently prepared for the journey that love requires.

The five wise maidens, however, realized that love is a journey, and by the very fact that they were sufficiently prepared by having oil with them, they were communicating to the bridegroom their commitment to the entire journey that their relationship with him would entail. Hence, they are considered wise, not only because they brought enough oil with them, but because they understood that any authentic and deep relationship consists primarily of two people journeying together and not simply seeking an immediate experience or feeling.

It would be worthwhile for us to prayerfully consider which group of maidens we belong to. The following questions can help us discern this more honestly: In our relationship with God, are we simply seeking an experience or feeling of him? Is our whole relationship with God based upon the hope that he will fix some immediate problem in our lives or remove any possible threat to our own happiness and comfort? How do we respond to God if we don't feel anything, or if God doesn't seem to answer our prayers in the way we believe is best? The answers to these questions will not reveal the state of God's love for us, since his love is always unconditional and remains the same. Rather, our answers to these questions will reveal the state of our love for God, something that unfortunately often changes because it is so often conditional.

Many people have confided to me over the years that they have stopped praying and attempting to live a spiritual life, not because they didn't believe it was necessary, but because most of the time they didn't feel anything or have any spiritual experiences. This always saddens me; however, I am quick to tell them, "*Neither do I, and neither do most people, and neither do most saints!*" Though there are objective criteria we can use to discern our relationship with God, we must never evaluate God's love for us and our relationship with him merely by feelings, consolations, or experiences.

In a deeply challenging passage St. John of the Cross alludes to this when he writes,

> It is noteworthy that, however elevated God's communications and the experiences of his presence are, and however sublime a person's knowledge of him may be, these are not God essentially, nor are they comparable to him . . . neither the sublime communication nor the sensible awareness of his nearness is a sure testimony of his gracious presence, nor are dryness and the lack of these a reflection of his absence.[11]

What St. John of the Cross is reminding us of is that the goal or purpose of the spiritual life is not to accumulate consolations and spiritual experiences. Rather, it is to give ourselves totally to God in faith, hope, and love, regardless of what our experience may be. Are consolations and spiritual experiences helpful? Yes, they can be very helpful. Does God give these things to people at times? Yes, he does, when he believes they will strengthen us and enable us to take the next step in our relationship with him. However, they are never given to us for the expansion of our own ego, or for us to waste time daydreaming about how holy we think we are because we have had certain experiences. If we do receive consolations and experiences from God, we should be humble, grateful, and receptive to them, yet we must not view them as ends in themselves or even as signs that we are progressing in holiness. Otherwise, the things of God, and not God himself, become the focus of our life.

It might appear silly to suggest this, however there is within our own humanity a grave temptation to approach God and the spiritual life as a means of self-promotion or for the fulfillment of our own will. Throughout human history people have used family, careers, physical appearance, and so much more as a means of self-promotion and for the fulfillment of their own will. Why then would it be any different in the spiritual life? After all, God does provide for our needs. God is concerned about our real lives and gives us grace to live them well. However, that's not all God does, nor is that all he is. Therefore, if we are only seeking an immediate experience of him, or expecting him to do what we want, when we want, and how we think best, then not only are we foolish, but like the foolish maidens in the parable, we may also end up missing God entirely!

Jesus concludes the parable of the wise and foolish maidens with a call to vigilance: *"Watch therefore, for you know neither the day nor the hour" (Matthew 25:13)*. Hence, to embark more deeply on this journey of love with God we need to practice vigilance and keep guard over our hearts and minds. Vigilance will keep us alert to our own innate tendency towards self-promotion and our own resistance to journeying with God in love. God is going to lead us beyond what we find comfortable, and beyond what we can understand with our minds. However, if we are only focused on ourselves, our experiences, and what we want, we will never be led into deeper intimacy with God. How could we? There is too much of us in the way!

Many of us will find ourselves at certain moments of our lives and even in certain moments of our days to be like the wise maidens, while in other moments we will be like the foolish maidens. When we realize that we are acting and living like the foolish maidens we must not be discouraged. God is using the awareness of our immaturity and the impurity of our love for him as a means of purification, so that our love for him becomes mature and pure. Hence, this is why our relationship with God is a journey, primarily a journey of purification of our selfishness so as to love others, and especially God, selflessly.

Are we willing to make this journey? Are we willing to give ourselves entirely to everything that this journey demands of us? If we truly and sincerely desire God, then the answer must be yes, so that like the wise maidens, we will not be caught off guard or lose faith if the bridegroom appears delayed. Rather, like them we will be prepared more fully for the journey that is our life with God.

14
God and Us

"While he was yet at a distance, his father saw him and had compassion, and ran and embraced him and kissed him."
—Luke 15:20

There is an inherent danger for us that is inscribed in the Parable of the Prodigal Son. Most people, I am sure, do not think of anything being dangerous about this famous parable. In fact, it is for most people the exact opposite. Over the centuries, this parable has brought hope, consolation, and joy to many, since the overwhelming theme of this parable is the unconditional love of God, symbolized in the love of the father who receives his wayward son back after the son abandoned his own family and made a mess of his own life. What then could possibly be dangerous about this parable? It is the fact that we know it so well.

Most of us have heard this parable countless times. We have prayed with this parable so often. We have read and listened to meditations on it. We have seen works of art depicting it, and we have probably spoken with others about it. Unfortunately, because we are so familiar with it, we have most likely taken it for granted. Its power and beauty can very easily escape us, not intentionally of course, but because we know it so well, at least on one level.

One day I was speaking with a priest friend of mine who is a Bible scholar. We were discussing this parable, and in the middle of our conversation my friend said that *"If the only piece of Scripture we had was the Prodigal Son, that would be enough for us, because it perfectly reveals to us the truth about God and us."* I remained in silence for a long time after my friend spoke those words and began to wonder if I really knew this parable as well as I assumed I did.

What then is the essential message of the parable of the prodigal son? What is God trying to tell us through the story of a younger son who has everything and out of utter selfishness and stupidity renounces his own family and then throws his entire life away, and then after he returns home, is not greeted with anger or punishment, and doesn't even experience justice, but instead is shown compassion, forgiveness, and mercy? There are, I believe, two essential messages to this parable.

The first message of this parable is that God is unconditional love. The phrase "unconditional love" is one that we often hear in sermons and in books. It is a phrase often used when evangelizing or attempting to explain Christianity to others. Yet, how do we understand unconditional love, and what does it really mean? The simple answer is, we can't understand it, at least not fully. Why? Because we have relatively little experience in this life of a love that has no boundaries or limits to it. We cannot understand, and we rarely experience, a love that never gets tired, a love that is constant and unchanging, that allows itself to be ignored, taken for granted, ridiculed, and then still says, both in word and action, *"I love you."* This is who God is, and what he is like.

Though this is clearly the message of the parable of the prodigal son, is it not also the main message of our own lives? Do we need this parable to know the truth that God is unconditional love? Well, yes and no. I would never suggest that this parable is not important for each one of us or that we do not need to meditate upon it and pray with it often, or that what it reveals is not necessary for us. However, if we look deeply enough at our life, I believe we can see the same message of this parable, not as a rare occurrence in our life, but as the consistent thread that runs through the entirety of our life. Think for a moment about your own conversion, reversion, or vocation. Maybe you are someone who has always been devout, maybe you are someone who has experienced a radical conversion at some point in your life, or maybe you are someone who is serving the Lord in the Church as a priest, a religious, or one who is involved in some sort of ministry.

Are we foolish enough to think, regarding our own conversions, reversions, or vocations, that it was our own strength, intelligence, or holiness that brought this about? If we do, then we are utterly foolish. Not only are we foolish, but we are completely blind and deaf to the presence of God and his voice in our life. This is so because our conversions, reversions, or vocations have nothing to do with our own initiative, regardless of how clever or intelligent we think we are. Rather, they have everything to do with God.

St. Paul alludes to this in a sobering way in his first letter to the Corinthians when he writes,

> Consider your call, brethren; not many of you were wise according to the flesh, not many were powerful, not many were of noble birth; but God choose what is foolish in the world to shame the wise, God chose what is weak in the world to shame the strong, God chose what is low and despised in the world, even things that are not, to bring to nothing things that are.
>
> (1 Corinthians 1:26–28)

At first glance, St. Paul's words can appear not only discouraging, but also rude. After all, he calls the Corinthians foolish, weak, low, and despised. If he were alive today, he would probably be forced to undergo "sensitivity training," or at the very least, take a course on how to be more pastoral in the modern world. Despite how St. Paul's words here might be interpreted by some, what St. Paul is intending to do is affirm the Corinthians, and us, with these words. But what is he affirming? He is not affirming that the Corinthians are independent, self-sufficient, and competent people who have their lives together and who need nothing. If we are honest, that is what most of us want to hear; however, as St. Paul reminds them, that is not true. So how then can this message be affirming?

St. Paul is reminding them that their conversions and vocations are simply the fruit of the unconditional love of God for them, something which is not dependent upon their being perfect or performing in a certain way.

The first message then of the parable of the Prodigal son is a revelation about who God is. The second message of this parable is a revelation about who we are, namely that we are sons and daughters of God. Throughout the entire parable there was never a moment when the younger son did not belong entirely to his father. Even though he rejected his family, *"squandered his property in loose living" (Luke 15:13)*, and spent all his inheritance, he was never, despite how he might have felt or even what he chose to believe, alone in this world or abandoned by his own family. He always had a home and he always belonged. There was nothing, not even his own stupidity, that could take that away from him—even though he tried desperately to be someone else.

One of the most beautiful experiences I have as a priest is receiving someone who has been away for many years from the sacrament of reconciliation. Often, when a person has not received the sacrament for many years, there is much in need of healing. Also, because they have not experienced God's mercy in the tangible way the sacrament reveals it, most of these people approach the sacrament afraid and worried that they are beyond hope, or that God is not going to forgive them. One of the things I always remind them of—and this is hard for all of us to believe regardless of how often we receive the sacrament of reconciliation—is that God never stopped loving them. In other words, God never changes the way he feels about us. He might not love our actions, attitudes, words, etc., but he never stops loving us, and the reason for this is that we are always his son or daughter. We have never been anyone else. Thankfully, there is no one else to be.

Over the years I have witnessed this reality with my nephews. Both of my nephews, when they were teenagers, caused a certain amount of stress and worry for my sister and her husband, as have many teenagers, including me. There was a particular period when one of my nephews, who was 17 years old, appeared to be ready to move out because of a high level of tension at home. There were constant arguments, hurt feelings, and many unkind words exchanged during this time. Shortly after this, I spoke to my nephew after one of his many arguments with his parents and asked him if he was planning on moving out. He responded simply by saying, *"I have nowhere else to go. This is my home and this is my family."* I was impressed that my nephew, who was only a teenager at the time, had such clarity about who he was and where he belonged. If only we had that clarity in our relationship with God!

There are some who may view this attitude as being merely a pastoral approach to ministry. In other words, this approach is a "dumbing down" of the faith or an elementary explanation to reach people and attract them to the gospel. This approach is neither: It is the gospel message in its fullness. St. John tells us in his first letter, *"See what love the Father has given us, that we should be called children of God; and so we are" (1 John 3:1).*

The implications of this truth in our life are liberating. So often we ask ourselves questions such as, "Who am I? What am I supposed to do and be in life? What is my purpose?" What the parable of the prodigal son reveals to us is that who we are and what we are supposed to be in life is merely a son or a daughter of God. There is no need to pretend we are anyone else. There is no need to try to hide behind or create an identity based upon our social status, apostolic success, worldly achievements, gifts, experiences (even spiritual experiences), or all the many other things in life. Being a son or daughter is all we need to be. It really is that easy, and this is the great secret both to life and holiness.

The Parable of the Prodigal Son provides for us the foundation of our relationship with God and a foundation for understanding who we are as well. If this foundation is not firmly established in our hearts and minds, we will not adequately be able to grow in a deeper relationship with him, nor will we ever be able to understand who we are. This foundation reminds us that God is unconditional love and that we are his sons and daughters. This is the beautiful and liberating truth of the gospel, which, thankfully, is meant to be the beautiful and liberating news of our own lives. Regardless then of how often we have heard this parable and how well we may think we know it, we must embrace its message anew so that we can enter more profoundly into the fullness of this good news.

15
Is Happiness Important?

"Blessed are the poor in spirit,
for theirs is the kingdom of heaven."
—Matthew 5:3

In his biography of St. Francis, G. K. Chesterton writes that "*If a man saw the world upside down, with all the trees and towers hanging head downwards as in a pool, one effect would be to emphasize the idea of dependence . . . for the very word dependence only means hanging.*"[12] Chesterton, in his quintessential paradoxical style, will deduce from this statement that it is when we are upside down, or at least see things upside down, that we see things right side up. Chesterton believed that one of the essential characteristics of St. Francis, and really of all the saints, was that they lived upside down and therefore saw everything as being dependent upon God.

Maybe the last time we were upside down was when we were a child hanging from a tree, doing cartwheels in the grass, or riding on a roller coaster. However long it has been for us, I would encourage you to imagine what the world looks like from this viewpoint. When one is upside down the whole world—trees, buildings, people, cars—appears as if it is hanging from the sky by an invisible string. Everything appears as it really is, dependent on something else not only for its existence but for its current state of being, since nothing is sustained by itself. And of course, that's the way things really are: Everything is dependent upon another, namely God. Therefore, to see things correctly we must be turned upside down.

Perhaps there is no piece of Scripture that turns us more upside down than the Beatitudes. If we read them merely on a surface level the Beatitudes are nothing else than a series of paradoxes that clash fiercely against worldly wisdom. When Jesus describes *"the poor in spirit . . . those who mourn . . . the meek . . . those who hunger and thirst for righteousness . . . the merciful . . . the pure in heart . . . the peacemakers . . . those who are persecuted for righteousness' sake" (Matthew 5:3–10)* as blessed, many of us are left scratching our heads and thinking to ourselves, *"How can such a person be considered blessed?"* After all, the world often considers blessed those who are strong, successful, and independent.

The Beatitudes are intentionally meant to turn us upside down so that we can see things correctly and therefore be turned right side up. How do they do this, specifically? They reveal to us what true happiness is and where it can be found.

One of the Franciscans with whom I lived in community spent the first thirty years of his life pursuing what the world told him would make him happy. He was physically strong and in robust health, he was a lawyer in a very successful firm, and for the most part, he came and went as he pleased. Despite all of this, he said, he never experienced happiness. In fact, the more he achieved what he considered the world's criteria for happiness, the more anxious, isolated, and sad he became.

Gradually over time, he began attending Mass during the week. On the feast day of a particular saint, the Gospel read that day was the Beatitudes. The priest said during the homily, *"The only truly happy people in life are the saints, not because they meditated on the Beatitudes, or considered them important, but because they lived them."* Those words became a moment of grace for my fellow Franciscan because they revealed to him two things. First, like the saints, he couldn't simply meditate on the Beatitudes. Rather, he needed to live them. Second, the path on which God was calling him to live the Beatitudes best was entering the Franciscans. Shortly after that day he quit his job, gave away everything he owned, and entered the Franciscans. Six months after we entered together and became novices and received our gray Franciscan habit, he turned to me with a huge smile and said, *"I am finally happy."*

The Catechism of the Catholic Church states that *"The Beatitudes respond to the natural desire for happiness."*[13] This statement should immediately get our attention, because happiness is something everybody desires. There has never been one person in human history who has said, *"I want to be miserable,"* yet everyone throughout history has said to some degree, *"I want to be happy."* It would not be an exaggeration then to say that the motivation of all people everywhere is the pursuit of happiness. Why is this so? Because God has placed inside the human heart the desire for happiness in the hopes that it would draw us to him, the only one who can fulfill this desire completely.

Interestingly, in my life as a Franciscan the most common question I receive from people, both religious and non-religious—including family members, people at doctor's offices and gas stations, strangers I may meet in a store, and even fellow priests and religious—is *"Are you happy?"* I can always sense when the question is coming, and I almost always dread hearing it. Usually, after I explain to a person the reason I am wearing my gray Franciscan robe is that I am a Franciscan priest who has taken vows of poverty, chastity, and obedience, there is an awkward pause in the conversation, while the person looks at me either in awe and amazement or with sorrow and pity for me. After they have recovered from my answer, they almost can't help themselves and ask, *"Are you happy?"* The reason I mentioned that I don't like hearing this question is not that I am unhappy. In fact, I consider myself a relatively happy person. It's the way the modern world tends to define and understand happiness that makes me uneasy.

One definition of happiness that I read recently was this: *"Happiness is an emotional state characterized by feelings of joy, satisfaction, contentment, and fulfillment."* Happiness, at least according to this definition, is being described essentially as a fleeting, constantly changing experience, that has no depth to it. If happiness occurs only when our emotions are in harmony and producing feelings such as contentment and fulfillment, then there will be very few happy people. Quite honestly, if this is all that happiness is then I don't want to be happy.

Jesus wants us to be happy, though his understanding of happiness is much different from the world's. Let us return to the Beatitudes. At their core, the Beatitudes are a portrait of Christ. It is only Jesus who fulfills each one of the Beatitudes perfectly. St. John Chrysostom writes that *"In every beatitude the blessed are receiving the kingdom of heaven."*[14] Hence, by proclaiming the Beatitudes and calling us to live them, Jesus is not offering us a philosophical or even a theological teaching. Rather, he is showing us that if we truly want to follow him and be his disciples, we must embrace the Beatitudes as the path of genuine discipleship. Why? Because by embracing the Beatitudes we are embracing him and becoming more like him. Even though the process of living the Beatitudes will turn us and our worlds upside down, it is the only happiness in life worth pursuing.

In short, real and lasting happiness is the fruit of genuine holiness, or, as St. Peter describes it, as becoming *"partakers of the divine nature" (2 Peter 1:4)*. What does holiness ultimately mean and look like? Quite simply it means becoming God-like. It means seeing as God sees, thinking as God thinks, and loving as God loves. When our hearts, thoughts, and actions are like God's, a natural consequence of this is happiness. The extent to which we are growing in genuine holiness will be the extent to which we experience genuine happiness. One of the main reasons for this is that the happiness that occurs through holiness is not fleeting like our emotions. The greater our holiness becomes, the greater our foundation and strength in God, who is unchanging, becomes.

Since the Beatitudes are the path of genuine discipleship, and therefore the path to real and lasting happiness, it could be helpful to use the Beatitudes as a weekly or monthly examination of conscience.

Every week or once or twice a month, one could spend a few moments prayerfully asking oneself, *How poor in spirit and meek have I been this month? How much have I hungered and thirsted for righteousness? How merciful and pure in heart have I been? How much of a peacemaker have I been?, etc.* The point of such an examination is not to make a person feel bad because they most likely have not responded perfectly to the gospel, but to help a person see where they may need to grow. This then can help a person enter more into a life of deeper holiness and greater happiness.

The world is not wrong in its pursuit and desire for happiness. Understood correctly, happiness is the purpose of our lives. However, true and lasting happiness cannot be reduced to a feeling, emotion, or experience. Nor can it be acquired totally and completely from anything of this world, even the good things of this world. True and lasting happiness can only come from God, the ultimate good. If we are united with him and live these Beatitudes, happiness will be ours in abundance.

16
The Necessity of Solitary Prayer

"In the morning, a great while before day, he rose and went out to a lonely place, and there he prayed."
—Mark 1:35

In the first chapter of the Gospel of Mark, the evangelist provides us with a window into what a day in the life of Jesus looks like. As one can imagine, it's quite busy. St. Mark records that after leaving the synagogue where he has cast out an evil spirit (Mark 1:25), Jesus enters the home of Simon, whose mother-in-law is lying in bed sick with a fever. Jesus immediately comes to her, takes her by the hand, and heals her. Shortly after we are told that the people of the area *"brought to him all who were sick or possessed with demons. And the whole city was gathered together about the door"* (Mark 1:32–33). Despite Jesus's attending to the multitudes, healing the sick, and exorcising demons, his apostolic work is not finished. The next day we are told that Jesus is preparing to move on to the surrounding towns to preach, and, one would assume, continue healing the sick and casting out evil spirits.

Yet despite all this busyness and overwhelming need we are told that *"In the morning, a great while before day . . . [Jesus] rose and went out to a lonely place, and there he prayed"* (Mark 1:35). How mysterious and beautiful is this verse and the reality that it signifies. Yet also, how strange it is. Why would the Second Person of the Holy Trinity need to pray? Why would he choose to step away for a time of solitary prayer, when it is very clear that so many people are in desperate need of him? The answer, I believe, is twofold.

First, Jesus knows that the entire universe is not only in the hands of the Father, but more importantly, it is in the Father's heart. Jesus will reference the Father's tender care for all of his children and his own trust and faith in the Father's goodness later in the Gospel when he says, *"Do not be anxious about your life, what you shall eat or what you shall drink, nor about your body, what you shall put on . . . your heavenly Father knows that you need them all" (Matthew 6:25, 32)*. Is Jesus dismissing the importance and necessity of apostolic work? Is he advocating merely a passive approach regarding the necessities of life, both for ourselves and others? Of course not. But what Jesus is reminding us of is an important truth that is meant to serve as the foundation for both our earthly life and ministry and our spiritual life. The truth is this: The Father is always caring and providing for us in every moment of life. If he were not, the world and we ourselves would not exist. Therefore, we do not have to be anxious, we do not have to kill ourselves by overworking, and most importantly we can enjoy time alone with the Father so as to marvel more deeply in his love, goodness, and providential care for all of us.

Second, Jesus understands prayer very differently than many people. For Jesus, prayer is not merely a means to get something from the Father. It is not an opportunity for him to try and show the Father that he is lovable, good, and faithful, and therefore the Father should give him whatever he asks for. Prayer is not merely an obligation that he is performing to fulfill the requirements for a proper relationship with God. Rather, prayer is an opportunity to intensify and deepen his union with the Father, to express his love for the Father, and to receive the Father's love more deeply. This is why Jesus seeks out times of solitary prayer. I have often believed that how a person understands prayer will ultimately reveal who they understand God to be. By seeking out times of solitary prayer, Jesus is revealing to us that the Father is not some cold, disinterested, transcendent being hidden away in another universe. Rather, God the Father is one who is near, affectionate, and interested in every detail of our lives.

To put it more simply, Jesus is teaching us that prayer is ultimately about love: receiving the Father's love and loving him in return. People who are in love never need an excuse to be together, especially when they desire to be alone. Love is the very reason for their solitude together. There is no explanation necessary.

The most characteristic trait of Jesus in the Gospels is that he is always seeking the Father. His only desire is to do the Father's will *(John 4:34)*. His primary mission is to reveal to the world the Father and his love *(John 14:9–11)*. Jesus's motivation for all the healings and exorcisms, and even his Passion, is to glorify the Father *(John 17:4)*. Naturally then, because the Father is who Jesus loves most, he will regularly seek out solitude with him. The frequency with which Jesus does this—and we see him do this all throughout the Gospels *(Matthew 14:23, Mark 6:46, Luke 6:12, John 6:15)*—reveals the intensity of his love for the Father. If we are to imitate Jesus, as all of us are called to, then we too must seek the Father with a similar intensity. To the extent that we seek the Father in solitary prayer, our love for him will be revealed.

It is important to acknowledge that prayer for most people does not begin with this solitary nature, at least usually. The more generous a person is in prayer, always in obedience to their state of life, the more deeply they will be led into this solitude, where they will seek to be alone with God more regularly. This does not mean that one must become a monk or a nun, or if they are married, ignore their families and their responsibilities, so that they can spend hours alone with God in prayer. Rather, this shift in prayer is more subtle. As a person begins to grow in their life of prayer, very gradually they will desire and begin to seek out opportunities to be alone with God, whether that be for five or ten minutes or an hour or two. The distinctive characteristic of this solitary prayer is not primarily to meditate upon God, as good and necessary as that is, but simply to be with him in greater love and receptivity.

St. John of the Cross teaches that there are three signs one should use to discern when a person can leave discursive meditation and pass on to the grace of contemplation, that is, contemplative prayer.[15] The third sign, which he believes is the most important, is the following: "*A person likes to remain alone in loving awareness of God, without particular considerations, in interior peace and quiet and repose, and without acts and exercises, (at least discursive, those in which one progresses from point to point) of the intellect, memory, and will.*"[16] Hence, a key sign of growth in our spiritual life is both the desire and the ability to be with God in solitary prayer. Furthermore, St. John of the Cross also teaches that it is in contemplative prayer that God performs the most purifying and healing work in a soul, which implies the absolute necessity of solitary prayer for us if we truly desire holiness.

The religious order that I belong to, the Franciscan Friars of the Renewal, is an active religious order, meaning that my community is engaged in various apostolic works that include things like hands-on work with the poor, preaching, and other forms of ministry. Throughout my religious life, I have worked with other apostolic religious orders and ministries in the church. During that time, I have listened to many people speak about the need to be generous in the apostolate and in fraternal life. However, in my own experience I have not heard many people speak about the need of being generous in one's life of prayer. Without generosity in prayer there can be little to no real generosity in the apostolate or fraternal life. The reason for this is that the demands of the apostolate and fraternal life are simply too much for us. They are beyond our natural strength.

Without a deep life of prayer, our apostolic life will possess a major problem: There will be too much of ourselves in it. Our preaching, helping the poor, and simply living the Christian life with others will contain too much of our own anxieties, fears, and insecurities. Of course, the grace of God can and does work through all of this. However, if we are to provide the world with the greatest possible Christian witness, then we need, as much as possible, a transfigured humanity, one that reflects and reveals the love and mercy of the Father. When we imitate Jesus and seek the Father more regularly in solitary prayer, this transformation is that much closer.

A few days before my ordination to the priesthood, I was on retreat at the seminary with my classmates. One morning I went to the cafeteria to get a cup of coffee, and an older priest, whom I had never seen before at the seminary, was doing the same. He asked me if I was one of the seminarians who would be ordained in a few days. I said yes, and he asked me to sit down with him for a few minutes and share some of my vocation story with him. As I was finishing my story, I asked him if he had any advice for me, since he had been a priest for over thirty-five years. He paused for a moment, looked out the window and said, *"It's great that you studied all this theology, but remember the world doesn't need theology, it needs God, and for your theology to have any impact in people's lives, you must meet the living God every day in solitary prayer. If you don't, nobody will listen to you, nor should they."*

After he had spoken those words the only place I could go was the chapel. I had always known that prayer was the most important aspect of my life and vocation. However, the words this priest spoke to me appeared not only as a confirmation of the importance of prayer, but also almost as a command from God himself. As I knelt in that chapel staring at the tabernacle, I sensed the Lord continuing the conversation by telling me, *"Your vocation is going to be difficult. Your intelligence, theology, religious order, and talents are not going to save you. Only I can save you and form you into the priest you are meant to be. However, if you don't spend time each day in solitary prayer, I can't help you."*

I have been a priest now for more than thirteen years, and those words I heard both from that priest in the cafeteria and from God in the chapel shortly before my ordination are truer than ever. There are new problems and difficulties in the world, in the Church, and even in my own heart. However, the more generous I am in my life of prayer, especially solitary prayer, the more intimately I experience the Father's love, goodness, and nearness to me. This prayer, the greatest treasure in my life, is not only for me. What I have received in those daily encounters with God in solitude I have attempted to share in all the many people my priesthood has served, and in all the varied ways God has willed. Though I am not always able to see the fruit of my ministry, I trust that God's grace is at work through me. One thing I do know is that without solitary prayer, I would lack the strength and trust to continue moving forward, because I cannot save myself or anyone else.

17
Our Point of Reference

"Follow me and I will make you become fishers of men."
—Mark 1:17

In one of his sermons, Meister Eckhart once said, "*Whoever seeks God and seeks anything with God, does not find* God . . . *for* . . . *if you seek God and seek him for your own profit and bliss, then in truth you are not seeking God.*"[17] What Meister Eckhart is hinting at here is a basic spiritual principle that we need to follow if we wish to deepen our relationship with Christ. The spiritual principle is this: To follow God more deeply we must let go of everything that is not God.

Upon hearing this we might not find it unusual or even radical. It is, after all, common sense, for if one were to say that they were truly seeking God yet were approaching him simply so that he could fulfill a list of personal requests and desires, the sincerity of that person's desire for God could be questioned. One could legitimately ask such a person, Do you desire God for his own sake or for yours?

Nonetheless, even though this spiritual principle may not be earth-shattering, it is rare to discover the essence of this principle alive in the hearts of human beings. The pure desire for God alone and the willingness to let go of everything for God are things we all must pray for. However, we must admit that many of us are not quite there yet.

This spiritual principle finds its origin and inspiration in almost every page of the Gospels. We could cite numerous examples in Jesus's words and actions where this principle is at work, but for our purposes here, I would simply like to take a brief look at Jesus's calling of the first disciples in the Gospel of Mark. When Jesus approaches Simon and Andrew they are fishing. Fishing is their livelihood; it is how they provide for themselves and their family. It is what they know best. In modern times, we could say it is their career. Yet Jesus says to them, *"Follow me and I will make you become fishers of men" (Mark 1:17)*. Simon and Andrew immediately let go of their nets, that is, their career and what they know most intimately, to follow Jesus. When Jesus approaches James and John they too are fishing, but when Jesus calls them, not only do they let go of their nets but also *"they left their father Zebedee in the boat with the hired servants, and followed him" (Mark 1:20)*.

On the surface, the call of these first disciples can appear very simple. St. Mark does not record any resistance, doubts, or discussion from the disciples regarding Jesus's invitation to follow him. In fact, it is quite simple, maybe even too simple for us to be able to relate to. Jesus calls them and they follow. However, we must consider for a moment what ultimately the invitation of Jesus to follow him consists of. Primarily, it is a call to Jesus himself. However, in this call is the invitation to Simon, Andrew, James, and John to let go of their identity and their security in this life. By letting go of their family they are ultimately letting go of who they have always known themselves to be. By letting go of their livelihood and careers they are letting go of their security. Why would Jesus ask that of them? Why does he ask this of us today? Is it because those things are bad? Of course not. Both family and career are very good, and they are often a means of grace and holiness for us.

These first apostles must let go of their family and career because Jesus wants to be their primary source of identity and security. Jesus wants to be their, and our, ultimate point of reference in life—not family, career, or things like our ethnicity, culture, health, talents, vocation, or anything of this world. Jesus, and Jesus alone, must be our only point of reference! This is his greatest desire, and it is the main reason he invites us to follow him.

Upon hearing this many people, both Christian and non-Christian, will ask, *Why can't my family, my career, or anything of this world be my ultimate point of reference?* The answer does not require a supernatural perspective. It can be answered simply by observing the nature of this world, which is summarized perfectly by St. Paul when he reminds us that *"The form of this world is passing away" (1 Corinthians 7:31)*. If our point of reference in life, our identity and security, are found in that which is passing away, how secure will we really be? How deeply will we really know ourselves and anyone else? And how happy could we honestly be?

Over the years I have spoken with many parents whose sons and daughters were in the process of entering seminary or religious life. In my own experience, about half of those parents adopted the opinion that if this is what will make my son or daughter happy, or if this is what they want to do with their life, then I will support them. About a quarter of those parents were angry at their child's decision and believed that they were making a grave mistake, and even in some extreme cases they expressed to their child their belief that they were wasting their life. The other quarter of those parents were overwhelmingly supportive and believed that their child's vocation was a gift and a grace not only to them, but also to their whole family, and this left them enthusiastic and supportive.

There is one family's response that I will never forget. A 25-year-old woman was entering a cloistered monastery. I had been this young woman's spiritual director for a few years and accompanied her through the process of her discernment to cloistered life. The rules of her community allowed her family to visit one time a year for a period of 4–5 days, and she would be able to call them only 4 times a year. Other than that, she would have no communication with them. Shortly before her entrance ceremony was about to begin, I was speaking to her father about his daughter's vocation and how it would change her relationship with her family. With deep humility and sincerity her father looked up at me with tears in his eyes and said to me, "*My daughter has always been God's gift to me. Now, I must give her back to him because she belongs more to Jesus than me.*" I was deeply moved by the sincerity, humility, and faith of this man. However, what struck me even more was not how profoundly he understood the Gospel, but how generously he was willing to live it.

To follow Jesus more intimately, Simon, Andrew, James, John, and we are being asked to let go of a lot, and this can seem at first overwhelming and frightening. And, on many levels it is! Yet we must ask ourselves, *What does letting go in the spiritual life really mean and ask of us?* Unfortunately, throughout the history of Christian spirituality certain terms in the spiritual life, such as *letting go* and even *detachment*, have acquired a negative connotation because the emphasis is placed upon what a person is losing. Thankfully, letting go is a positive reality, not primarily because of what one is losing, but because of who one is receiving. Letting go does not mean that I must reject someone or something, or that I must deny them or even become repulsed by them and consider them not worthy anymore of my love, attention, and affection. Rather, letting go in spiritual terms always implies releasing the grip or hold I might have on something or someone.

Why must I let go of the hold that I might have on something or someone? So that I can give more time, energy, and love to Jesus. So that I can be led entirely by him and give my whole self to him. By doing so, my faith, hope, and love for him and in him will grow exponentially, and in turn I am allowing myself to be led more deeply by him. None of this can occur if we are holding on to anything or anyone else, even the good things of this world.

We know from the Gospels that after Jesus calls these first disciples, this will not be the last time they ever go fishing. In fact, after the Resurrection Peter himself proclaims to the disciples, "*I am going fishing*" (*John 21:3*), to which the other disciples with him, including James and John, respond by saying, "*We will go with you*" (*John 21:3*). Also, we can assume that James and John would see their father again as well. Yet, after they have begun to follow Jesus, fishing and their family will be different for them, because they are different. With Jesus as their primary point of reference, they will be able to love their family, their careers, and the good things of this life appropriately. Because when we let go of everything that is not God, everything mysteriously ends up in its proper place, and they—and we—end up eventually losing nothing and gaining everything.

The faith and trust that are required of us to get to this point are enormous, and we cannot underestimate this. In the spiritual life it is often normal that a person takes two steps forward and one back. In other words, we progress very slowly, mostly because our humanity is often timid and even fearful before the transcendence and mystery of God. Thankfully, God is extremely patient with us and continues to invite us to let go of whoever or whatever we may be holding on to. More specifically, he continues to invite us to find our complete identity and security in him alone. Can we trust God enough to let go of everything that is not him? If we can, then like the disciples, we will experience both the joy and the freedom of leaving everything to follow Jesus.

18

Responding to Hypocrisy

"He who is greatest among you shall be your servant."
—Matthew 23: 11

Several years ago, after celebrating Mass in Manhattan one Sunday morning, I left the church and began walking towards the subway. Out of the corner of my eye I saw a man who appeared very angry rushing towards me. As he got about ten feet away from me, he began to yell, *"Father, I am leaving the Church."*

The crowds continued to walk past him without even seeming to notice him. I stopped, turned around and began to walk towards him. When I approached him, I introduced myself and attempted to shake his hand. However, before I could even finish, he said again, though this time sounding even angrier,

"Father, I am leaving the Church."

"Before you do that," I said to him, *"tell me why you are leaving the Church."*

Without any hesitation he responded, *"I'm tired of all the hypocrisy, scandals, lies, and corruption."*

I responded immediately, *"So am I!"*

Appearing somewhat shocked by my response, he seemed to relax a bit, paused for a moment, and then said to me, *"Why don't you leave the Church and become a minister in another church or do something different in your life?"*

I smiled at him and said to him very sincerely, *"Do you honestly think that there is another church or place in this world where there is not hypocrisy, where there are not scandals, lies, and corruption?"*

After I said this, we sat down on the sidewalk and spoke for about 30 minutes. He, like many people, had been hurt by certain members of the Church. All I could do was listen, apologize for the sins and mistakes he encountered among some members of the Church, and remind him that even though there are hypocrites in the Church, there are also many good people striving for holiness, and that the Church, like every institution, is a collection of both saints and sinners.

I tried to remind the man that not only are hypocrisy and scandals not something unique to the modern church, but they were also something that Jesus encountered among the religious leaders of his day, and that he warned us we would encounter also. Thankfully, Jesus has left us sound advice not only on how to respond to hypocrisy, but also on how to protect ourselves from falling prey to it.

Shortly before Jesus is about to begin his Passion, he says to the crowds, *"The scribes and the Pharisees sit on Moses' seat; so practice and observe whatever they tell you, but not what they do; for they preach, but do not practice" (Matthew 23:2–3)*. Jesus affirms that the scribes and Pharisees have been given authority to teach the Mosaic Law and proclaim God's word, hence they are seated on the chair of Moses. The problem, however, is they don't practice what they preach, and they use their authority for self-serving means. *"They do all their deeds to be seen . . . they love the place of honor at feasts and the best seats in the synagogues, and salutations in the market places" (Matthew 23:5–7)*. Interestingly, despite the Pharisees' and scribes' obvious hypocrisy and the scandal they cause, Jesus never condemns their message or denies their authority. Instead, he warns the disciples, and us, not to follow their example of hypocrisy.

What exactly is a hypocrite? A hypocrite is a person who says one thing and does another. He is, in a sense, two different people, or at the very least an extremely divided person. Hence, the image he attempts to display is essentially a false one, because his actions contradict the image he means to convey. Therefore, a hypocrite is not an authentic person. However, before we start finger-pointing at all the people in our life who fit this definition, if we are honest we must admit that there is a hypocrite within each one of us. I have never met one person in my life, especially me, who practices perfectly what he preaches. Again, this is not a justification for the damage a hypocrite can cause, but simply a reminder that *"all have sinned and fall short of the glory of God" (Romans 3:23).*

There is then nothing new about hypocrisy. It is as old as humanity itself, and therefore naturally it finds its way even into religion. However, the worst kind of hypocrite, that is, the one who can cause the most damage and scandal, is a religious one, because a religious hypocrite is essentially using God and the things of God for his own advantage and glory. However, not only are such persons using God, but they are also taking advantage of other people, specifically the vulnerability and trust with which a person who is seeking God manifests to a religious leader. The damage that can occur because of this is awful and must be eradicated as much as possible.

The Pharisees and the scribes exemplify then what false or bad religion looks like. Rather than simply telling us how we should not act, Jesus concludes this section by describing for us what true religion is meant to look like if we desire to be authentic disciples. Jesus says to the crowds, *"He who is greatest among you shall be your servant" (Matthew 23:11).* The distinguishing mark of authentic discipleship is, according to Jesus, the giving of ourselves. The hypocrite only serves himself, and therefore he is filled with self-love, whereas the authentic disciple, following the example and the commands of Jesus, goes out of himself to serve others.

Therefore, if we really want to know how authentic our discipleship is—again, none of us are perfect here—we can simply ask ourselves, how deep is our gift of self to God and therefore to others? Perhaps these few questions can help in discerning the authenticity of our discipleship. How deep is our gift of self to God in a life of prayer? In the service of my neighbor? In the performing of my daily duties and responsibilities that are part of my vocation? The reason this is important is that holiness does not occur somewhere else than in the very real circumstances and situations of our lives. Holiness, practically speaking, means living ordinary life in an extraordinary way. When we are living our ordinary life in this way, the risk of hypocrisy is greatly lessened within us, because it is God and others we are serving and not ourselves.

The greatest witness to a life of self-giving love to God and others, and therefore the greatest source of inspiration for us, can be found in the lives of the saints. The saints of every time and culture encountered hypocrisy in the world, the Church, and life in general. How did the saints respond to hypocrisy? Did they leave the Church to start a new one? Did they abandon Christianity and faith in Jesus because of the bad examples of some of those who claimed to be his followers? Did they stop praying, receiving the sacraments, and meditating on the Word of God? The saints did quite the opposite. In fact, the hypocrisy they encountered caused them to enter more deeply into the life of the Church and therefore the Christian faith. Rather than become discouraged by the bad example of others they pursued a life of holiness, that is, a life of self-gift as opposed to the self-love of hypocrisy. In short, the saints responded to hypocrisy with holiness.

In the fourth century after Christianity became legal and shortly afterward was declared the official religion of the Roman Empire, Christianity became in certain sections lukewarm and carried with it certain social benefits that Christians had never experienced before. Now that Christians were no longer being martyred for their faith, Christianity was safe, comfortable, and in some sense, even politically correct. Though none of this is intrinsically bad, one of the natural consequences of this is that a greater amount of hypocrisy began to occur among some of its members. Seeing the danger of what was happening to the Christian faith, St. Anthony of the Desert and some others decided that rather than be discouraged by the bad example of certain Christians, they would chose to embrace the gospel more deeply by moving to the desert to live a life of prayer, fasting, and penance. Hence, the lives of the Desert Fathers and Mothers emerged, because one person, St. Anthony, decided to respond to hypocrisy by pursuing a life of holiness.

A similar example can be seen during the period of the Reformation and the Counter-Reformation that followed. During the fifteenth and sixteenth centuries the Catholic Church needed great reform. There was much hypocrisy, scandal, and corruption in the Church. Although many left the Church during this time, some chose to reform the Church and respond to the hypocrisy that was occurring, not by leaving the Church, but by immersing themselves more deeply in it through a greater gift of self to God and his people. St. Ignatius of Loyola, St. Charles Borromeo, St. Teresa of Avila, and many other saints were raised up during this dark time in Church history because they chose to respond to hypocrisy by personal holiness.

Those who have responded to hypocrisy with holiness, whether it be the Desert Fathers and Mothers, the saints of the Counter-Reformation, or the thousands of other souls throughout Church history, have left us not only an inspiring example from the past but also a blueprint to follow in the current culture and climate that the Church faces. The past 25 years for the Catholic Church in America have been very difficult for everyone. There have been many scandals, lies, and examples of corruption that have been exposed for all to see. The Church has a responsibility to ensure this hypocrisy never occurs again.

However, we must not assume that the power to stop hypocrisy lies only among the Church leaders and the members of the hierarchy. Throughout Church history, most of the people who effected the greatest change both in the Church and the world were not its leaders. Rather, the greatest change has always occurred through simple and ordinary people whose love for God inspired them to make a greater gift of themselves. How then will you and I respond to the hypocrisy we encounter in the world, the Church, and even in ourselves and among our own families and friends? If you and I are not sincerely pursuing holiness, then we are not part of the solution, and therefore we shouldn't complain. The saints, following the teaching and example of Jesus, remind us that the only adequate response to hypocrisy is holiness.

19
God Is Now

"As he walked by the sea of Galilee, he saw two brothers,
Simon who is called Peter and Andrew his brother,
casting a net into the sea; for they were fishermen."
—Matthew 4:18

One day a terrible fire destroyed a monastery. Completely devastated, the monks gathered the next morning with the abbot in what was left of their chapel. The looked around in disbelief that what was once such a sacred space for their relationship with God was now for the most part reduced to ruins. The abbot suggested that the monks pray together in the chapel regardless of the condition that it was in. Once the monks had finished praying, there was a deafening silence that filled the ruins of the chapel. The youngest monk, who was sitting next to the abbot, cried out, "*Father, what are we going to do now? Our chapel is destroyed, our hermitages are unlivable, and even the chapter room where we have our weekly meetings and discussions is wrecked. We cannot live our monastic life in these conditions. The whole reason why I came here no longer exists.*" The abbot paused for a moment and assured the young monk and the other monks that they would rebuild the monastery and that God would provide everything they need.

A few months passed by and the monks, with the help of many volunteers, were able to rebuild their monastery, move back into their hermitages, return to the chapel for liturgy and prayer, and continue living their quiet monastic life. Shortly before Easter the bishop arrived on a Saturday morning to bless the rebuilt monastery and rededicate their chapel. While they were outside waiting for the procession to begin, that young monk said to the abbot, "*I am so relieved. Finally, after so many months of waiting and hard work, I will be able to pray again. I will be able to meditate on God's word and listen more deeply to God and once again live my vocation. I can finally be a monk again.*"

The abbot immediately turned to him and said with the utmost seriousness, "*My son, what have you been doing during these past months while we were working? Were you not praying? Were you not meditating on God's word? Were you not listening to God? Were you not living as a monk?*" The young monk looked confused and even embarrassed as the abbot continued, "*My son, God is in the present moment. If you cannot live there, you will never find him regardless of what your vocation is.*"

I believe what the abbot was trying to teach this young monk is an important spiritual truth that all of us need to be reminded of, whether we live in a monastery or not. The truth is this: God is now. Despite all the external features and conditions of one's life that would appear to make God's presence impossible and even amid the imperfections one may find in others or in oneself, none of this is an obstacle for God. God is present to us anyway, right now.

This truth is revealed in a subtle way in the calling of the first disciples in the Gospel of Matthew. We are told that Jesus is walking by the Sea of Galilee and that Peter, Andrew, James, and John are fishing. During an ordinary day of work for these disciples, Jesus calls them and says to them, "*Follow me, and I will make you fishers of men*" *(Matthew 4:19)*. As beautiful and profound as Jesus's words are to them, what is equally beautiful and profound, and I would argue quite astonishing, is where Jesus calls them. These first disciples are not in the temple praying. They are not at home in their study or prayer corner meditating on the Word of God. They are not living on some mountain removed from the anxieties and pressures of daily life, nor are they sitting at the feet of a wise and holy person.

What are these disciples doing when Jesus comes to them? They are working! Specifically, they are casting nets into the Sea of Galilee because they are simple fisherman. On a surface level there is nothing extraordinary or necessarily spiritual about what these disciples are doing, and yet it is in the context of their ordinary, daily life that Jesus enters and calls them. In other words, the present moment for them becomes the place where they will encounter the presence of God. In fact, the present moment, regardless of what that might look like or even feel like for a person, is always the place where God is and therefore where an encounter with him is always possible. We see this truth all throughout Scripture.

Matthew encounters Jesus while he is working (Matthew 9:9). Mary Magdalen meets Jesus while she is grieving and weeping at the tomb (John 20:15), St. Paul while he is persecuting Christians (Acts 9:4), the Samaritan woman as she is drawing water (John 4:7). Simon's mother-in-law encounters Jesus while lying in bed sick with a fever (Mark 1:30). There are of course many other biblical examples that illustrate this point. However, what is so radical and life-changing about this is that none of this looks very "spiritual"—and for all practical purposes it's not. These disciples, in their encounter with Jesus, are not at their physical or even spiritual best. They are in many ways unprepared and *"anxious and troubled about many things" (Luke 10:41)* that are not specifically related to God. Yet what these encounters teach us is two things. First, Jesus is not waiting for us to attain a certain degree of holiness before he reveals himself to us. Thank God! Second, the place where he reveals himself to us most regularly is our normal life, that is, the present moment. Therefore, the more deeply we can live in the present moment, again regardless of what the exterior conditions of it are, the more deeply we can be aware and live in the presence of God. Why? Because God is now!

One of the greatest experiences in this life is being surprised by God in the present moment. Every one of us has had these experiences. In fact, if we sincerely reflect upon our life, each one of us will be able to recount many instances where God's presence became known to us in the ordinary moments of our daily life. Perhaps we were by ourselves walking on a country road, or maybe we were having lunch with a friend, or maybe we were sitting quietly in church gazing upon the crucifix or the tabernacle, when suddenly God's presence became very tangible for us. I'm not suggesting that we heard voices or had visions, but rather in the quiet recesses of our hearts we became aware, for a moment, more deeply of God's presence. It is almost as if God interrupted our life for a moment just to remind us, *"I'm here, you are not alone."*

A friend of mine who lives in a beautiful part of the country recently shared with me an experience she had driving through the mountains at sunset. The sun was resting perfectly upon the snow-covered mountains, radiating a beautiful glow across the horizon. As my friend continued driving towards the sunset, its beauty became more visible to her, and tears began to roll down her face for no apparent reason. Suddenly, she said, she began to weep profusely, not because she was sad or having a difficult day, but purely because the beauty of the mountains and the sunset led her into a tangible experience of the beauty of God. I asked her what she was doing before that experience occurred, and she told me she had just came from church where she had spent an hour in Eucharistic adoration. When she asked me what I thought of her experience, I shrugged my shoulders and said to her with a smile, *"Maybe God wanted to remind you that he was still with you!"*

Experiences of God's presence in our ordinary life, like those mentioned above, are purely gifts of God's grace. There is nothing we can do to make these experiences happen. They are yet another reminder of God's love for us and his continued presence in our lives. Why do I believe that these experiences are among the greatest that we can have in life? Because they remind us that our lives and God are not two separate realities. If we really want to find God and live deeply with him, then outside of the liturgy and sacraments, all we must do is live deeply in the present moment with faith in God, because that is where God is. The present moment is always where God is waiting for us.

Faith then is the key that unlocks the depth and beauty of the present moment and enables us to experience more acutely God's presence. In the spiritual classic *Abandonment to Divine Providence*, Jean-Pierre de Caussade writes that "*Every moment reveals God to us. Faith is our light in this life. By it we know the truth without seeing it, we are put in touch with what we cannot feel, recognize what we cannot see, and view the world stripped of all its superficialities. . . . Faith tears aside the veil so that we can see the everlasting truth.*"[18]

The sign then of real growth in our spiritual life is not specifically the experiences, feelings, or insights that we might have during prayer, all of which of course are important. Rather, the greatest sign of a mature spiritual life is a maturing life: a life where we are becoming more loving, patient, and forgiving, and where we are more willing to trust God beyond what we can see and understand simply with our own humanity. The training ground for this maturity is the present moment, since this is where God most assuredly is. In fact, the spiritual life, our relationship with God, doesn't exist anywhere else than in the present moment, because the present moment is the only place where each one of us can be right now. Therefore, it is also the place where God is for us right now. Hence, when we can live the present moment in our ordinary lives with faith in God's presence, we will become more and more pleasantly surprised to discover this important and necessary spiritual truth: God is now!

20

Following Jesus to Eternity

"Those who are accounted worthy to attain to that age and to the resurrection from the dead neither marry nor are given in marriage, for they cannot die any more."
—Luke 20:35–36

For many people eternity is only an occasional thought. Perhaps it is inspired by the death of a loved one or the experience of sickness, or is simply the fruit of aging. What we are usually consumed by is our life in this world, what we are going to eat for supper, how we are going to manage our money, where we are going to go on vacation this summer, and so many other worldly questions and concerns.

God, on the other hand, though concerned about our life in this world, is mostly consumed by the reality of eternity for each one of us. St. Paul reminds us of this when he says, *"each one of us shall give account of himself to God" (Romans 14:12)*. Therefore, *"If for this life only we have hoped in Christ, we are of all men most to be pitied" (1 Corinthians 15:19)*. It would be impossible then to understand St. Paul, and especially the gospel, without this eternal perspective in mind.

It is worth asking ourselves, *Is eternity something that I spend time each day meditating on? Do I allow the reality of eternity to form my thinking, influence my decisions, and even evangelize my emotions and feelings? Does the reality of eternity increase my desire for prayer and the willingness to grow in virtue?* Why must we daily place ourselves before the reality of eternity? Primarily because it is our destiny at the end of the temporary pilgrimage that is our life in this world.

Several years ago, I gave a talk at a parish, and afterwards I stood at the door to say goodbye to all those who attended. A man, most likely in his 50s, pulled me aside and asked to speak with me in private. He retired, he told me, when he was forty years old after working on Wall Street for only ten years. He asked if I could recommend any charities to which he could donate a large sum of money. After I mentioned a few different organizations that do tremendous work with the poor and suffering, I asked him how much money he was intending to donate. When he told me the amount, I assumed I had misheard him, and when I asked him again, he repeated the same amount. I was shocked and said to him, "Are you sure you want to donate that much?" Immediately, he responded, "This life is so short, Father. I can't take all this money with me to eternity, so I might as well make good use of it while I am here now." This man, I was convinced, thought regularly about eternity, and by doing so his life in this world was properly ordered.

St. Augustine reminds us that *"The sole purpose of life in time is to gain merit for life in eternity."*[19] Nonetheless, despite our best efforts, none of us can adequately prepare for eternity by ourselves. To do this, each one of us must allow Christ to lead us beyond this world. We do this best not only when we ponder his word and seek his presence in our lives, but also when we surrender ourselves wholeheartedly to him.

Throughout the Gospels, Jesus is often seen in conversation and quite often in tension with a Jewish group known as the Sadducees. The Sadducees, often translated from Hebrew as "righteous," were an elite and aristocratic school of belief within Judaism. They denied the resurrection of the dead and the existence of angels and the soul, and only accepted the Torah (the first five books of the Bible also known as the Pentateuch) as authoritative.[20]

There is an episode in the Gospel of Luke (20:27–40) where the Sadducees attempt to discredit Jesus's teaching regarding eternal life by presenting to him a dilemma based upon Moses's teaching (Deuteronomy 25:5) found in the Torah. The dilemma is this: If a man's brother dies and has no children, that man must take his deceased brother's wife and raise up children for his brother. However, if the first brother marries her and dies childless, and the same thing happens to the second, third, fourth . . . all the way up to the seventh brother, then if there is a resurrection from the dead, whose wife will this woman be, since all seven were married to her? The Sadducees hope that this exaggerated story will not only undermine Jesus's teaching regarding eternal life but also his reputation as a holy and wise teacher. In many ways, their strategy and even their argument is a good one, from a purely earthly perspective.

However, Jesus responds to them, *"The sons of this age marry and are given in marriage; but those who are accounted worthy to attain to that age and to the resurrection from the dead neither marry nor are given in marriage" (Luke 20:34–35)*. Jesus's response to them is startling, and they are not prepared for it. Eternity, Jesus is reminding the Sadducees and each one of us, is unlike anything we can fathom. There are no analogies and metaphors that we can use from this life that will ultimately give credence to the reality of eternal life. Why? Because God is unlike anything we can fathom.

Furthermore, what Jesus is trying to do is not merely to correct their thinking, but to open their hearts to follow him. Why? Because in him eternity is present and speaking to them. In Jesus eternity is revealing itself and breaking into this world and calling each one of us beyond it. St. Catherine of Siena once famously said that *"All the way to heaven is heaven, because Jesus said, 'I am the way.'"* Hence, if we are sincerely following Jesus, if our hearts and minds are open to him, and we are listening to his Word and his presence in our life, then we are to some extent already living in eternity. Heaven then is not a question but a reality in which to some degree we are already participating. This is why the ultimate answer to the Sadducees' question is Jesus. He is the answer that can't merely be taught and accepted in a formal and academic way. Rather, he is the answer that must be believed and lived in the depths of one's heart.

There are many great questions that all of us face in life: Who is God? What is heaven like? How do I pray? It is necessary that we seek answers to these questions from wise and holy people, from good books, and even from our own soul searching. However, all these resources, as good and necessary as they are, have their limits. What all of them can do is point us towards the truth. They cannot bring us into the truth. If we believe that Jesus is *"the way, and the truth, and the life" (John 14:6)*, then the only way we can be brought into the truth is through discipleship, through a greater surrender to Jesus and a deeper following of him in our whole life. Teachers, books, retreats, and spiritual conversation are all helpful; however, they are not enough. Ultimately, we must leave the comfort and even the consolation of books, retreats, and spiritual conversations and follow Christ wherever and however he is leading us.

This is evidenced so clearly in the life of the disciples as recorded in the New Testament. When Jesus appears to two of his disciples after the Resurrection on their walk to Emmaus, he upbraids them for their lack of faith: *"O foolish men, and slow of heart to believe all that the prophets have spoken!" (Luke 24:25)*. The disciples here are not simply having a bad day, nor is this is an isolated event. All throughout the Gospels we witness the disciples' lack of faith. We see them arguing with each other about who is the greatest *(Luke 9:46)*, we witness Peter denying Jesus *(Luke 22:57)*, and much to our horror we see Judas betray Jesus for thirty pieces of silver *(Luke 22:5, 48)*. There are many other examples we could use from the Gospels to illustrate the disciples' weakness and their spiritual immaturity. However, the point is already made clear: These disciples are not yet saints. There is still something necessary they lack.

However, after the Resurrection there is an extreme transformation that has occurred among the disciples. *The Acts of the Apostles* records that after Pentecost, these same fearful and weak men are no longer hiding and running away from the crowds. Rather, they are now publicly proclaiming the gospel everywhere. What has happened to them? First, their encounter with the risen Lord has calmed their fears and quieted their anxieties regarding the true nature of Jesus. Second, the descent of the Holy Spirit has enlightened their hearts and minds by helping them to understand more deeply the mysteries of faith. However, these occurrences, as necessary as both are, are not enough to bring about this transformation. Something else is needed.

What is needed from the disciples is a personal yes to the presence of Jesus. Jesus, for them and for us, cannot remain an object of curiosity or fascination, or even a "what if" hypothetical question that we entertain occasionally in our minds. To experience the reality of who Jesus truly is, a person cannot only meditate upon his words or consider him in times of quiet and prayer. They must, as best they can, put these words into action, and allow his presence to carry them through this life and beyond it to eternity. The significant difference between a disciple of Jesus and one who is not, is that a disciple no longer spends time wondering if Jesus's words are true, and considering the possibility that he may be God. Rather, a disciple orients his entire life around the presence of Jesus, who he knows is God, and anchors his life in the truth of his word.

The problem with the Sadducees, specifically in the Gospel passage we reflected on earlier, is that they are attempting to interpret life, the Scriptures, and God apart from Jesus. By their doing so, all their answers will be incomplete. To understand life, the Scriptures, and God we must lay aside what we think and understand and give ourselves entirely to Jesus. As we do this, not only will he reveal the truth to us about these realities and so much more, but also he will take us beyond ourselves and this life to eternity.

21
The Cost of Discipleship

"Even the hairs of your head are all numbered."
—Matthew 10:30

There is a famous story about St. Teresa of Avila that reveals both her strong character and God's playfulness. One day as St. Teresa was traveling around Spain attempting to reform various monasteries, the wheel of her carriage hit a rock and sent St. Teresa flying out into the rain-soaked mud. Frustrated and annoyed, St. Teresa looked up to heaven and said to Jesus, "Don't you see all that I am trying to do for you?" To which she heard Jesus respond to her, "Teresa, this is how I treat all my friends." St. Teresa replied without any hesitation, "Well, it's no wonder you have so few!"

This story can be consoling for us because it reveals the humanity of the saints. If the saints can get frustrated and annoyed, then there is hope for the rest of us! However, hidden within this story is a subtle temptation to think that if we are following Jesus and seriously pursuing a life of holiness, we will be exempt in some way from the ordinary sufferings of life such as becoming sick, falling into a puddle of mud, breaking an arm or a leg, or even experiencing emotional or psychological sufferings. As nice as this wishful thinking may be, Jesus never makes such a promise.

If a Christian is not promised to be spared the ordinary sufferings of life, then one could legitimately ask, what difference does Jesus make in life? If I am going to suffer with Jesus or without Jesus, what is the point?

The answer to this apparent dilemma can be found in chapter ten of the Gospel of Matthew. In this chapter, often referred to as the "great commissioning," Jesus sends out his disciples to preach the gospel. After instructing the disciples what to do, namely, to preach, heal, and cast out demons (Matthew 10:7–8), and after warning them that they will experience persecution, Jesus teaches the disciples about the one thing that will greatly inhibit not only their missionary life but also their interior life: Fear! *"Have no fear of them,"* Jesus says, and *"Do not fear those who kill the body but cannot kill the soul" (Matthew 10:26, 28).*

One could read these words of Jesus and conclude that the reason he tells his disciples and us not to be afraid is that nothing bad is going to happen to us. If only that were true! A few verses earlier Jesus warned the disciples, *"I send you out as sheep in the midst of wolves. . . . Beware of men; for they will deliver you up to councils, and flog you in their synagogues, and you will be dragged before governors and kings for my sake" (Matthew 10:16–18).* Shortly after Jesus's admonition to have no fear he says, *"Do not think that I have come to bring peace on earth. . . . For I have come to set a man against his father, and a daughter against her mother . . . and a man's foes will be those of his own household" (Matthew 10:34–36).*

Sandwiched in the middle of these promises of persecution is Jesus's admonition to *"have no fear."* How strange is it that Jesus warns us about persecution, tells us not to be afraid, and then continues to warn us about more persecution? Jesus is never one to sugarcoat anything, but one might conclude he is joking here. How can someone, even the holiest among us, not respond with at least some degree of fear, since fear appears to be the natural and appropriate response to what Jesus has assured us we will experience in living and preaching the gospel?

To answer this question adequately it is important to keep in mind that Jesus's primary mission and teaching is not to promise us earthly success or happiness or to make us feel good. Jesus has no desire to be politically correct or worldly minded, or to tell us what we want to hear. Rather, his primary mission and teaching is geared towards the salvation of our souls, something that very often contradicts political correctness and worldly thinking, and doesn't always appeal to our feelings and our human desires. In short, Jesus never assures the disciples that everyone will accept them and listen to them, and that they will always feel affirmed and loved.

These challenging words of Jesus and the sobering reality that they foster are just as relevant and true for us today. According to the *Open Doors World Watch List 2022*, in 2021 a greater number of Christians were either detained or killed for their faith and more churches were attacked or closed than in 2020. 360 million Christians, or 1 in 7 believers around the world, suffered significant persecution for their faith. Every day in 2021, an average of more than 16 believers were killed for following Jesus. In 2021 alone there were close to 6,000 martyrs, which was a 24% increase over the previous year.[21]

Considering all this, one could be left to wonder, *Where is the good news here?* Or, to reiterate our question from earlier, *What difference does Jesus make?* The difference, though it may appear subtle and to some even unimportant, is immensely consoling and is the epitome of good news. Despite all the sufferings and trials we face in this life, Jesus tells us not to be afraid, because regardless of what happens to us in this world we are known and loved by God the Father. Furthermore, at this moment, not only are we are in the hands of the Father, but we are in his heart as well. If we are sick or dying, if we have been betrayed or treated unfairly, if we have been misunderstood, criticized wrongly, or treated unjustly, we are still known and loved, and we remain in the hands and heart of the Father. This good news that only Jesus can give us is something no person, no circumstance, and no situation in this world can ever take from us, unless of course we let it. Jesus emphasizes this when he tells us, *"Even the hairs of your head are all numbered" (Matthew 10:30).*

I suspect that if we are honest, we find this truth consoling, but many of us may be left wondering, *Why can't we have the best of both worlds? Why can't we be rich, healthy, and loved by everyone and have no problems or sufferings in life, and still love God and go to heaven?* The short answer to that question is, you can! However, God does require that he be our priority, not only because that is right and just, but also for the simple reason that if one had all those things—a life without suffering—one would most likely forget about God and seek satisfaction and fulfillment either in oneself, another person, or the things of this world.

As disciples of Jesus, regardless of our vocation in this life, we can be guaranteed that we are going to suffer and experience at least some degree of persecution. If God did not *"spare his own son" (Romans 8:32)* from suffering, why would he spare us from it? When suffering does come our way, we must be willing to carry our cross in whatever form it might take and unite it with Christ. After all, Jesus tells us, *"If any man would come after me, let him deny himself and take up his cross and follow me" (Matthew 16:24)*. By willingly choosing to embrace our crosses and unite them with Christ, not only are we obeying Jesus's commands, but also we are walking perfectly in the footsteps of the master.

Nonetheless we can and should always pray for healing, the end of suffering, and the removal of certain crosses in our life and in the lives of others. However, most of the time it seems that Jesus does not remove suffering from our lives. If he chooses not to, we must not view this as a punishment or conclude that we are doing something wrong, but rather as the ordinary path of discipleship that is necessary for us to walk if we wish to grow in genuine holiness. What I have noticed in my own life is that if God removes a certain cross or suffering in my life, rather quickly—sometimes in a matter of hours—another one appears. Depending upon the nature of this new cross, sometimes I find myself asking God to trade this new cross in for the one I was just begging him to remove!

What then is the implication of all we have been considering? In Matthew 10 Jesus is outlining for us what I like to call the cost of discipleship. If you want to be a disciple of Christ, you must give up your life. If you are a disciple of Christ, both you and your life are not your own. St. Paul reiterates this when he says, "*You are not your own; you were bought with a price*" (*1 Corinthians 6:19–20*). This does not mean that one cannot enjoy success, prosperity, and the things of this world. It is merely a reminder that you belong to God, and your life as a disciple is meant ultimately to be Jesus's life lived in, through, and with you. To put it more simply, a Christian's entire life, from the most minute detail to the most significant, is meant to reveal, glorify, and proclaim God.

When I was a child, my dream was to become a professional baseball player. When I was a teenager, it was to be a musician, and when I first started college, it was to be either a philosophy or a literature professor. None of those dreams came true, and I thank God every day that they didn't. Instead, I have discovered something greater: God's dream for my life, specifically to be a Franciscan priest. My vocation has brought me a joy and a peace that none of my dreams ever could have, and with each new day God's dreams for my life continue to unfold.

Every one of us has dreams for our life. This is good and even necessary. But what about God's dreams for our life? Does God not see more than I do? Does God not know more than I do? Do we trust him with our life? This is really the crux of discipleship: surrendering our dreams and our wills to God in exchange for his dreams and his will for us.

The Christian life, despite how some may understand it, is not an escape from reality, but is quite honestly the only way through reality. In the Gospel of John, Jesus says, "*I lay down my life. . . . No one takes it from me, but I lay it down of my own accord*" (*John 10:17–18*). Jesus is leaving us an example here not only to marvel at, but also to imitate. If we wish to live our lives well as disciples, we have no other choice but to do the same. This indeed is the cost of discipleship, but its investment will reap eternal rewards.

22
The Simplicity of Prayer

"This is my beloved Son; listen to him."
—Mark 9:7

If I were to ask a room full of people what one of the easiest things there is to do in life, there would most likely be as many different answers to that question as there are people. For some, the answer might be cooking, reading, or sleeping. For others it might be spending time with friends, playing a sport, or doing something creative and artistic. Very few people, I believe, would say that prayer is one of the easiest things there is to do in life. As surprising as this answer might appear, it is true. There is nothing easier than prayer, at least in theory. Ironically, because prayer is simple and relatively easy, this is also one of the reasons why it can be so difficult for us.

Throughout history many theologians, saints, and ordinary people have provided various definitions of prayer for us. Each one of us, I would imagine, if we were asked what prayer is, would be able to provide our own definition based upon our knowledge and experience of prayer. The way I personally understand prayer is this: regardless of the various form of prayer one is engaged in, at its core prayer is a loving gaze upon God in faith, through which we are drawn more and more into God's presence, his life, and his love. This is what ultimately changes our hearts, our minds, and eventually our lives.

Consider for a moment the Rosary, lectio divina, the Jesus prayer, or any other form of prayer. What do all these have in common? They are all attempting, through different means, to draw us more deeply into the presence, life, and love of Jesus by helping us focus our gaze upon him. The more deeply our gaze is upon him, the more our love and faith in him will increase. The reason for this is that when we allow ourselves to gaze upon Jesus, we encounter his overwhelming beauty, love, and mercy, at which even the most hardened heart will begin to soften.

I have met people throughout the course of my priesthood who tell me that they pray several Rosaries a day, do other pious practices, and even attend daily Mass, yet they experience little to no transformation in their life. Whenever I hear this, I immediately respond by asking them: *In prayer are you lovingly gazing upon God in faith, or are you mostly talking at God?* If the answer is the latter, then of course they will experience little to no transformation even if exteriorly they are participating in good and holy things. The reason there is no transformation is that they are not allowing themselves to be draw more deeply into God's presence. Therefore, they never really end up being with him and resting in his presence, because they cannot settle their gaze upon him.

We can witness all these dynamics that are involved in the life of prayer in the Gospel account of the Transfiguration. The Transfiguration is a significant event in the life of Jesus that is mentioned in each of the Synoptic Gospels (Matthew 17:1–13, Mark 9:2–8, Luke 9:28–36). It has enormous theological and biblical implications, and, as I will attempt to show, it has enormous spiritual implications for us as well, specifically regarding our life of prayer.

Pope St. John Paul II, in his apostolic letter on the Rosary, says,

> The Gospel scene of Christ's transfiguration . . . can be seen as an icon of Christian contemplation. To look upon the face of Christ . . . this is the task of every follower of Christ. . . . In contemplating Christ's face we become open to receiving the mystery of Trinitarian life, experiencing ever anew the love of the Father and delighting in the joy of the Holy Spirit.[22]

The more often and deeply we gaze upon Christ in faith, the more deeply we are led into the mystery of God.

In the event of the Transfiguration, Peter, James, and John are invited into this extraordinary experience of Jesus. They witness "*his garments . . . glistening, intensely white, as no fuller on earth could bleach them,*" and they see "*Elijah with Moses . . . talking to Jesus*" (Mark 9:3–4). The disciples have a front row seat to this remarkable theophany of God. In Mark's account of the Transfiguration, we are not told how James and John responded; however, we are told one thing specifically about Peter: he can't keep still. Peter cannot keep his gaze upon Jesus. He can't savor and rest in this profound moment and gift that is being given to him. He must start planning and even trying to control God's revelation. During this extraordinary experience Peter proclaims, "*Master, it is well that we are here; let us make three booths, one for you and one for Moses and one for Elijah*" (Mark 9:5).

Peter's suggestion to Jesus sounds good, pious, and even holy. However, deep prayer is not the time for one's own ideas and plans, even for spiritual plans that appear good and holy. What is it the time for? Stillness! Stillness both exteriorly and interiorly so that we can be drawn more deeply into God's presence, otherwise we may interfere with the grace that God wishes to bestow upon us in this profound time of grace. St. John of the Cross teaches that for a soul who is advancing on the path of contemplation, that is, deeper prayer, their spiritual directors should not "*impose meditation on persons in this state, nor should they oblige them to make acts or strive for satisfaction and fervor. Such activity would place an obstacle in the path of the principal agent who, as I say, is God.*" For a person thus experiencing the grace of deeper prayer, St. John of the Cross recommends that these people "*should proceed only with a loving attention to God . . . without efforts of their own but with the simple, loving awareness, as when opening one's eyes with loving attention.*"[23]

In short, we respond most deeply to God in prayer by intensifying our gaze upon him and becoming receptive to this grace so that we can receive from this moment whatever God desires to bestow on us. In Matthew's account of the Transfiguration, he confirms this when he recounts that it is while Peter "*was still speaking . . . a bright cloud overshadowed them, and a voice from the cloud said, 'This is my beloved Son . . . listen to him'" (Matthew 17:5)*. It's as if the Lord is saying to Peter, "This is not the time for your plans and ideas, because something greater is occurring."

Ultimately, Peter cannot listen to Jesus and receive fully the gift of Jesus, because his gaze is scattered. His heart and mind are distracted and busy with his own plans and ideas and probably his own worries and fears as well. This then is the reason that prayer is difficult for us at times, because like Peter we are interiorly divided and therefore unable to keep our gaze upon Jesus for very long. The less we keep our eyes on Jesus, the more scattered, distracted, and anxious we will become.

In the life of prayer, we will encounter many twists and turns and moments of illumination and moments of darkness. We will experience consolation and God's grace in tangible ways at times, but we will also experience dryness and desolation. If we persevere in prayer, we will even feel at times that God has abandoned us and that we are completely alone in this world. Though these realities might surprise some people, this is what the life of prayer looks like for anyone who takes it seriously. If a person imagines that prayer will always give a sensible or emotional experience of God, or that the saints and mystics always experienced God's light and love in extraordinary measures each day, then that person does not know the saints or spirituality well, nor have they themselves prayed deeply yet.

Is prayer then simple and easy? Despite all the challenges that we will face in the life of prayer, it remains one of the easiest things we can do. As we experience various challenges in our prayer life, we will have to discern certain exterior dynamics to our prayer. Just as in life "*there is a season, and a time for every matter under heaven" (Ecclesiastes 3:1)*, so too in the life of prayer there is a time for everything. For example, it is necessary that we meditate upon God's word regularly.

However, there will also come the time when we can't meditate on God's word because the Lord is calling us to simply rest in his presence in silence and stillness. After a certain time of silent prayer, the Lord may be preparing a soul to do some intense interior work on an emotional and psychological level that will require of a person a more active and conversational form of prayer. This then could lead back to greater silence in prayer or even to a particular devotion conducive to a person's specific situation. I have never met even one person who prays the exact same way for their entire life. Those who grow the most deeply in prayer are those who let go of their own desires in prayer and follow the way in which the Lord is inviting them to pray. In all of this we must beg God, *"Lord, teach us to pray" (Luke 11:1).*

However, regardless of how one is praying exteriorly, whether it be with the Scriptures, a devotion, or in silence, one thing that can never change in prayer is this fundamental posture of prayer, to be lovingly gazing upon God in faith. When prayer is dark and difficult it is very easy to take our eyes off God and focus more on the darkness and emptiness we may be feeling. Or if the Scriptures are not nourishing us as they once did, it is very easy to focus more on the desolation we may feel, rather than on God's presence. If we are experiencing any of this we must stop and ask ourselves, *Where is my heart? Is it, like Peter, distracted and busy with my own desires, plans, and ideas? Is it, like Martha,* "anxious and troubled about many things" (Luke 10:41)*?* The answer to this question might not eliminate the darkness we are experiencing in prayer, but it will reorient our minds and hearts back to the Lord, since they have most likely strayed from his presence.

No matter what our experience in prayer may be, each time we begin we must once again refocus and intensify our gaze upon Christ. The more often we do this, and the longer our gaze upon Christ remains, things like darkness and desolation will not affect us as greatly. This is because, as St. Paul reminds us, *"Love bears all things, believes all things, hopes all things, endures all things" (1 Corinthians 13:7).* Hence, it is this loving gaze upon God in faith that not only heals us but also strengthens us to persevere in our life of prayer. By doing this we will know more deeply that even if we are not so simple, prayer is. The knowledge and experience of this will begin to draw us more deeply into Jesus and his transfigured glory.

23
Our Purpose in Life

"Be perfect, as your heavenly Father is perfect."
—Matthew 5:48

I was recently speaking with a friend of mine who is a psychologist. During our conversation, he told me the greatest suffering that he encounters among people today is that so many people are living without a purpose for their life. According to my friend, many people are drifting through life without any awareness of why they are here, and therefore they are unsure of how to live their lives. He explained that, at least psychologically—and this would be true spiritually as well—without a purpose and plan for one's life, a person's whole being begins to dissipate. In extreme cases one almost reverts to being an adolescent, becoming childish in one's behavior and thinking. Such persons drift along on the surface of life seeking their own satisfaction and pleasure, and therefore they never engage seriously with life and with others. It is obvious then what will occur next: They never grow up, because they perceive no purpose for their life beyond themselves and therefore they cannot live life appropriately.

The consequences of this can be quite serious, as my friend encounters almost daily among his patients. However, this situation would be even worse if the purpose for our life was a secret that was never shared. If this were the case, humanity would be destined to a life of misery, because there would be no transcendent meaning for our lives, and we would be forced to spend our entire existence trapped within ourselves. This is something, of course, that is a recipe for misery.

Thankfully, the Bible has always been very clear about what the purpose for our life must be. In his Sermon on the Mount, Jesus says these challenging words: *"Be perfect, as your heavenly father is perfect" (Matthew 5:48)*. What is this perfection that Jesus calls us to? It is holiness. The Old Testament expressed it this way: *"You shall therefore be holy, for I am holy" (Leviticus 11:45)*.

The purpose in life is holiness, and therefore the plan for our life must be for us to become holy. There is nothing greater in this life that one could achieve than holiness, since this is what we are made for, and it is ultimately the only place where our satisfaction, healing, and peace can come from. Hence, the pursuit of holiness is the one thing needful for all of us *(Luke 10:42)*.

The word *holiness* and the reality it signifies is for many people both an abstract and an archaic notion. It is necessary then that we understand holiness properly if we wish to understand the purpose for our life adequately. Generally, the biblical understanding of holiness is "that which is set apart or is sacred." When applied to God, *"The term holiness . . . denotes his innermost, secret essence, his mysterious, ineffable being which is totally distinct and separate from creation."*[24] Hence, God is holy, that is, he is totally other than this world.

There are two basic principles that flow from this. First, our call to holiness is an invitation to a personal encounter with God throughout our life. Second, because of this encounter, and especially as this encounter becomes more regular and deepens within us, we become more and more purified of that which is not God in us. In summary, since God is holiness itself, our growth in holiness is a participation in his holiness, that is, in God himself.[25]

As fascinating as the holiness of God is, what is also fascinating is the fact that holiness will look different in each one of us. Hence, there are no identical twins before God. This can be evidenced in the lives of the saints, those holiest people in whom holiness looked very different and was expressed very differently in each one. For example, St. Anthony of the Desert was a hermit who lived in solitude. St. John

Paul II was a pope who traveled the word extensively, preaching the gospel. St. Thérèse of Lisieux was a cloistered nun who never left her convent, whereas St. Teresa of Calcutta spent most of her days in the streets caring for the poor, sick, and dying.

What then does holiness look like in you and me? Only God knows; however, that question and the reality it signifies are worth pursuing and planning our entire life around, since holiness is the purpose of our life. The Church affirms this universal call to holiness when she states that "*The Lord Jesus, divine teacher and model of all perfection, preached holiness of life to each and every one of his disciples without distinction. . . . It is therefore quite clear that all Christians in any state or walk of life are called to the fullness of Christian life and to the perfection of love.*"[26]

St. Paul echoes these sentiments as well when he writes, "*This is the will of God, your sanctification*" *(1 Thessalonians 4:3)*. Even though holiness is the will of God for us, it does not happen without our consent. God never forces himself upon anyone. "*Behold,*" Jesus says in the book of Revelation, "*I stand at the door and knock; if anyone hears my voice and opens the door, I will come in to him and eat with him, and he with me*" *(Revelation 3:20)*. How will we use this remarkable gift of freedom that God has given us? If we wish to live authentically and not misuse the gift of freedom, then we must use this gift primarily for the pursuit of holiness.

Every day we must ask ourselves these questions: *Will I live this day purely for myself, seeking what I want, what I desire, what I think is right, etc.? Or will I live this day seeking God's will, his desires, and what he has revealed to be true?* Most of us are probably caught somewhere in between: One day or even one moment we are living purely for ourselves, then in the next moment or later in the day our hearts are oriented once again back to God and living for him.

Since holiness does not happen to us naturally, it is important that we pray each day not necessarily for the grace to become holy, since this is already the will of God for us, but for the grace to respond and cooperate with God's grace in our lives. If we embrace God's will fully in our lives, we will become holy, as the spiritual classic *Abandonment to Divine Providence* teaches: *"In reality, holiness consists of one thing only: complete loyalty to God's will."*[27]

It is easy to become consumed with one's own needs and desires and even how we think holiness is supposed to look in our life. We must be careful in prayer that we are not merely praying only for our own success or that things will go our way and with the least amount of annoyance and suffering for us. Of course, it is not wrong to pray for our own success. However, there is no real holiness occurring if we are just asking God to conform us to our plans, desires, and ideas of holiness. Nor is there any real holiness occurring if we are just asking God to conform himself to our plans, desires, and ideas of holiness. The pursuit of genuine holiness begins when we leave ourselves behind completely and embrace God totally!

In the Sermon on the Mount Jesus teaches us that *"If any one strikes you on the right cheek, turn to him the other also; and if any one would sue you and take your coat, let him have your cloak as well; and if any one forces you to go one mile, go with him two miles. . . . Love your enemies and pray for those who persecute you" (Matthew 5:39–41, 44)*. Through these seemingly absurd statements, Jesus is teaching us that a radical love for others is not merely a suggestion or something that will make us look good. Rather, it is an essential condition for holiness, since this radical love not only unites us to Jesus but also makes us like him *(John 13:34)*. Jesus is the One who has turned his other cheek (John 19:3). Jesus is the One who has been pressed into service and gone the extra mile *(Mark 15:20)*. Jesus is the One who has loved his enemies and prayed for his persecutors (*Luke 23:34*). Hence, the only adequate way we can understand the Sermon on the Mount, and all of Jesus's teachings in general, is through the lens of God's purpose and plan for our life, which is nothing else but the perfection that can only be found in a life of holiness.

The French novelist Leon Bloy once said that *"Life, in the end, has only one tragedy: not to have been a saint."*[28] At the end of our life, what will it really matter how successful we were in our careers, what people thought of us, or how big our house was? The answer is simple: none. If we believe that the purpose of our life is to seek material gain or personal satisfaction, or even to acquire a certain amount of notoriety and fame among our peers and those we encounter daily, not only will we be disappointed and continually restless, but also we will be missing the sole reason for our lives. Not only that, but if we believe that our life has no purpose and we spend our days drifting aimlessly from one experience to another without seeking any transcendent purpose to our lives, then our life truly becomes not only a shame, but also a tragedy.

I have been privileged to accompany a few people as they were dying. I have noticed that one of the greatest regrets from people in their last days is how much time they wasted in this life on superficial pursuits and concerns. The regrets I have heard have varied, but they all have one thing in common. One man admitted to me how much time he regretted working because, as he said, he placed his career ahead of his family, and unfortunately, he was never able to make up for the time he lost with them. A woman in her fifties spent her last moments regretting never forgiving her sister for something childish that happened over twenty years ago, and this had prevented her from even knowing where her sister lived. Another man I was with admitted to me that if he had spent half as much time on his spiritual life as he did on his hobbies, he would be dying a different person.

All these stories, and the many others I have witnessed, reiterated to me a singular theme: Holiness must be the priority of our lives. For this to occur, we must constantly be guarding our hearts and our minds from that which is vain, superficial, and worldly. If God is truly the holy one, present in though totally distinct from this world, then our thoughts, actions, and desires must rise above this world so that our lives can reflect and participate in the holiness that belongs to

God. When we attempt to do this, not only will we live well, but also we will die well, and we will most assuredly hear Jesus say to us at the end of our life, "*Well done, good and faithful servant . . . enter into the joy of your master*" (*Matthew 25:23*).

24
Zeal for Worship

"Making a whip of cords, he drove them all, with the sheep and oxen, out of the temple; and he poured out the coins of the money changers and overturned their tables."
—John 2:15

The biblical account of the cleansing of the temple is recorded in all four Gospels (Matthew 21:12–13, Mark 11:15–19, Luke 19:45–46, John 2:13–22). In this episode we encounter what can appear like a "different" Jesus than maybe the one we prefer or the one most often portrayed in the Gospels. However, the same Jesus we witness driving out with a whip those who were selling things in the temple and overturning their tables is the same Jesus who eats with tax collectors and sinners (Matthew 9:11), who heals the blind (John 9:1–12), the deaf (Mark 7:34), and the lame (John 5:1–9), and who forgives prostitutes (John 8:11), sinners (Luke 5:20), and even those who crucified him (Luke 23:34).

How then do we understand both Jesus's attitude and his actions in this Gospel passage? Before we attempt to answer that question, it is important to remember that to interpret any passage of the Bible sufficiently we must have a general understanding of the Bible as a whole. We must be aware not only of the basic story of the Bible, but also of its overall meaning and purpose. At the very least we must know what the Bible is ultimately revealing to us.

To understand then more adequately Jesus's actions in the episode of the cleansing of the temple, we must be aware of what the Bible indicates is his primary mission. Jesus's mission is revealed in many places, but especially in his conversation with Philip when he says, *"He who has seen me has seen the Father" (John 14:9)*, and also in the high priestly prayer when Jesus says to the Father, *"I made known to them your name, and I will make it known, that the love with which you have loved me may be in them, and I in them" (John 17:26)*. Jesus's mission is clear: it is to reveal the Father, not only who he is but also what he is like. Therefore, when Jesus is eating with tax collectors and sinners, he is revealing to us the Father's goodness and love for everyone. When Jesus heals the blind, the deaf, and the lame, he is revealing to us that the Father is our healer who not only cares for us but also knows us even in our physical condition. When Jesus forgives prostitutes, sinners, and even those who crucified him, he is revealing the Father's mercy and forgiveness.

Finally, we can now ask ourselves, what is Jesus revealing about the Father in the cleansing of the temple? He is revealing the holiness and transcendence of the Father, and therefore the right worship that is due to him. Jesus reveals to us that the Father is not some nice teddy bear up in the sky nor some exalted human being, nor is he simply one God among many. Rather the Father, Jesus reveals, is *the* God, the one God, the Creator and Savior and Lord and Master of everything that exists. Is it any wonder then that Jesus is outraged about what is occurring in the temple? They have turned the temple, the place of worship, the place where the holiness of the Father is meant to be reverenced with such sincerity and love, into, as Jesus describes it, a marketplace. Instead of coming to the temple to worship God, they are worshiping themselves and the things of this world. This obviously is gravely offensive to the Father and therefore to Jesus as well, which is why his anger towards those selling things in the temple is both right and just.

However, Jesus's actions in the temple are not merely an attempt to win a theological and liturgical war against his opponents. The temple personally for Jesus is a sacred place where his own intimate relationship with the Father is strengthened and affirmed. It was in the temple that Joseph and Mary presented him 40 days after his birth *(Luke 2:22–39)*. It was in the temple that at the age of twelve Jesus decided to remain and to remind his parents that he must be about his father's business *(Luke 2:46–49)*. Each year during his hidden life Jesus, at least for Passover, would go to the temple *(Luke 2:41)*, and it was in the temple that Jesus would often teach and slowly begin to reveal himself *(Luke 21:37–38)*. For Jesus then the temple was not only a sacred place where the holiness of God would be revered, but it was also the privileged place for his own relationship with the Father. Therefore, the temple was most especially a place of reverence, intimacy, and prayer for Jesus.

Before we proceed further it is important to have an accurate understanding of what worship is and what authentic worship is meant to look like in our individual lives. *The Catechism of the Catholic Church* defines worship as *"adoration and honor given to God,"* indicating that the worship of God is first and most important an act of the virtue of religion.[29] The reason for this is simple: Because he is God, the creator and savior, Lord and master of all that exists, he deserves worship. For us then to worship God is to acknowledge our absolute dependence upon him. It means that we must humble ourselves to praise and exalt, not ourselves or others, but God. Interestingly, the worship of God is our saving grace because it sets us free from turning in on ourselves, becoming slaves of sin, and falling into the idolatry of the world (CCC paragraphs 2096–2097).[30]

Herein lies an indisputable fact about the human person that is evidenced throughout history: Wherever there is not the worship of God there will be the worship of something or someone else. The human heart is not sufficient unto itself. It desires and needs to give itself completely to another. The other, who is in the end the only one sufficient for the human heart, is God. Therefore, the worship of God is meant to be not only our heart's natural tendency, but also its lasting fulfillment and peace.

Throughout history the worship of God, if not completely forgotten or ignored, has rarely been seen as a priority or as the one activity in life that gives the greatest depth and meaning to one's life. If one were to spend only five minutes either watching the news, or scrolling the internet, or perusing social media, one would find blatantly obvious what the world worships: sex, money, power, and a whole slew of other things that generally have the self and the experience of pleasure as the goal and fulfillment of life. All these things, of course, are totally inadequate and insufficient, both for us and, most importantly, for God. Jesus reiterates this to Satan in the desert in the final temptation: *"You shall worship the Lord your God and him only shall you serve" (Matthew 4:10).*

What about us then? Is our body—which, as St. Paul says, is a temple of the Holy Spirit *(1 Corinthians 6:19)*—a busy marketplace where we are buying and selling many things? Is it a place where the worship of God is seen not merely as an obligation, but its very joy and privilege? Is there anything that Jesus would remove from our hearts today so that we can worship the Father with greater purity and love?

In the first volume of the *Philokalia,* St. Isaiah the Solitary provides us with a challenging and sobering definition of worship. He says that to worship God we must *"have nothing extraneous in our intellect when we are praying to him: neither sensual pleasure . . . malice . . . hatred . . . nor jealousy to hinder us as we speak to him and call him to mind."* What St. Isaiah the Solitary is concerned with is not that one merely fulfills a moral precept. Rather, he is attempting to lead us towards purity of heart so that God can be worshiped adequately and we in turn can be transformed by our worship of God. He continues, *"For all of these things are full of darkness; they are a wall imprisoning our wretched soul, and if the soul has them in itself it cannot worship God with purity. They obstruct its ascent and prevent it from meeting God; they hinder it from blessing him inwardly and praying to him with sweetness of heart, and so receiving his illumination."*[31]

If we truly desire to live a life of greater worship of God, then the first step in this process is removing from our hearts any traces of darkness or division that exist within us. We must not be foolish to think this is something we can do simply by our own strength. Without the grace of God and our cooperation with it, none of us will be able to worship God with the purity and sincerity that he deserves. We must invite Jesus into the dark places of our hearts and minds, the places where malice, hatred, unforgiveness, pride, lust, etc., exist. However, inviting him there is not enough. We must, as strange as it may sound, give him permission to pour out and overturn anything within us that is hindering the worship that is due to God.

At the monastery where I served as a chaplain for three years, many of the retreatants would often remark to me how beautiful and uplifting they found the liturgies at the monastery. After attending either Mass or one of the hours of prayer, many of them would tell me they would often return to their hermitage with a great desire for prayer, because their hearts were aflame with the love of God. After hearing this comment so often I began to consider what specifically is so beautiful about the liturgy there. The sisters, to their credit, spend much time studying liturgy, practicing chanting, and choosing some of the most beautiful hymns and psalm tones available in both the Eastern and Western church. However, one could hire professional musicians to do the same thing, and though it would sound beautiful something essential would be missing. What would be missing is the purity and holiness of the sisters who lead the liturgy. And this, I believe, is what makes the liturgy at the monastery exceptionally beautiful.

Though there are certain external rubrics that need to be followed for the proper worship of God, it is ultimately the interior disposition of a soul that gives God the greatest worship. "*The sacrifice acceptable to God is a broken spirit; a broken and contrite heart, O God, you will not despise" (Psalm 51:17)*. Those who were doing business in the temple were doing something that was offensive and therefore highly inappropriate in such a sacred place. However, what these actions reflect is an interior disposition of one whose heart and mind are very far away from the love of God and the worship that is due to him. If we wish to worship God, both as he deserves and as our hearts ultimately desire, we must strive to purify our interior life. By doing so we will be demonstrating the zeal for worship that Jesus desires of us, and which will finally set us free.

25
Am I Resisting or Receptive?

"He will put those wretches to a miserable death, and lease the vineyard to other tenants who will give him the fruits in their seasons."
—Matthew 21:41

The parable of the wicked tenants (Matthew 21:33–43) can elicit many different reactions within us. It is easy to experience the beauty and grandeur of salvation history as one meditates on this parable; however, one can also experience the challenge this parable poses. After all, salvation history is *the* story, God's story of his plan to save us from sin and death despite ourselves, because we all know that God's love is rarely, if ever, met with perfect receptivity and unwavering faith. The one exception to this of course is Our Lady (Luke 1:38).

What then does salvation history look like from God's perspective? Jesus answers this question through the parable we are considering. God, the householder, creates all that is. He chooses Israel, a small and insignificant nation, as his vineyard. He puts people in charge as tenants of this land and entrusts to them the mission to make the God of Israel known. However, when harvest time comes God sends his servants the prophets to the tenants, Israel's leaders, to obtain his produce. However, Israel's leaders beat, kill, and stone the prophets. Finally, God sends his son, Jesus, thinking Israel's leaders will respect and listen to the son. But of course they do not, and they have him crucified. Hence, the drama of salvation history.

Through this parable Jesus is reiterating to us the grave responsibility that comes with the gift of God's grace. What is grace? It is God's life, given to us freely and undeservedly. Without God's grace there is no salvation history, since we are completely incapable of saving ourselves. Therefore, our responsibility to the gift of God's life to us is not to get in the way of it, not to resist it, and not to become an obstacle to it. In simple terms, our responsibility towards God's grace is to say yes to it and allow God to save us.

Israel's leaders throughout salvation history, and this would be equally true of leaders throughout Christendom as well, have been at times an obstacle to the grace of God, for themselves and therefore for others, which is why Jesus concludes this parable with these condemning words to them: *"He will put those wretches to a miserable death, and lease the vineyard to other tenants who will give him the fruits in their seasons" (Matthew 21:42)*. These are strong words, and as mentioned earlier, challenging and sobering words. However, they are not meant only for Israel's leaders 2,000 years ago. They are, in fact, meant for anyone who resists God's grace, because they emphasize the absolute necessity of our cooperation and receptivity to the grace of God in our life. St. Augustine sums this up perfectly when he reminds us, *"God who created you without you, will not save you without you."*

The seriousness of Jesus's words forces us then to ask ourselves: How am I responding to God's grace in my life? Where might I be resisting God's grace? Basically, am I resisting or am I receiving? If I am resisting, then I am resisting the very way in which God is trying to save me, heal me, and make me holy.

For most of my priesthood, I have been involved in spiritual direction, something which I consider both a joy and a privilege. Spiritual direction, at its core, is meant to accompany a person in their relationship with God. The desired end of spiritual direction is not simply friendship between two people, as good as that is, but growth in holiness of the directee. Therefore, a spiritual director's primary responsibility is helping a person to grow in holiness. How does a spiritual director do that? Not by projecting his own spirituality, his life experience, or even his own relationship with God onto the directee, but by simply listening to the directee and helping them to pay attention and then respond to God's grace in their life.

In spiritual direction there are two fundamental questions that must always be addressed in every meeting. The first question is, *What has God been like since the last time we met?* Specifically, *How do you perceive God to be acting in your prayer, daily life, or ministry?* The second question follows from the first: *How are you responding to God's presence and his grace in your life?* There appear to be only three possible answers to this question: I am either resisting God's grace, or I am receptive to it, or I am doing a little bit of both. In many ways this second question is more important because God's presence and grace in our life always call us to a response. This response does not necessarily imply that one must begin a new apostolic endeavor or make some major change in our life, though it certainly can include that. On a more holistic level our response to God's presence in our life might include something like a different way of thinking, a greater interior openness to another person, or living with a greater spirit of thanksgiving, repentance, or trust.

The importance, however, of responding to God's grace in our life is meant to be not only for us, but for others as well. Since no man is an island, my resistance or receptivity to the grace of God will in turn affect others to some degree. For example, imagine a mother or a father who has been experiencing in their soul the inspiration to return to the Church. Even though this grace is aimed directly at them, it will naturally affect those in their immediate surroundings, for example their children. If this mother or father says yes to this grace and returns to the Church, then most likely they will bring their children with them. Their children will in turn be nourished by the Word of God, receive the sacraments, and experience Christian community. However, if this mother or father says no to this grace, then they will in turn deny that grace not only to themselves but to their children as well. An elderly priest I know, who deeply understands this reality, once said to a father of three teenage boys, "If you're not going to come back to church for yourself, at least come back for your kids!"

The parable of the wicked tenants then reminds us that our life ultimately comes down to a singular choice. Will we be receptive to God's grace in our life, or will we resist it? Hidden within this choice is an important spiritual truth that all of us need to consider regularly, especially in moments of dryness, suffering, and doubt. God is giving each one of us the grace right now to respond to him. Regardless of what our vocation is, what the present circumstances may be, and even our own history, God is present to us right now, both with his love and his grace. His presence in each one of our lives is an invitation to continue walking with him in our own personal story of salvation. However, to experience God's love and grace more deeply in our life and therefore to walk on the path of our own salvation, we must say yes to this grace daily.

St. Paul experienced this in a rather profound way throughout his life. On one occasion he describes having been *"given . . . in the flesh, a messenger of Satan, to harass me"* (2 Corinthians 12:7). After he begged the Lord three times to remove this difficulty Jesus responded to him by saying, *"My grace is sufficient for you"* (2 Corinthians 12:9). Hence, Jesus was reminding St. Paul, as he always reminds us, that God's grace is never lacking in our life in any situation, even when that situation entails sufferings and trials. What is often lacking is our receptivity to this grace.

We witness this truth in the life not only of St. Paul but also of all the saints. The saints do not belong to simply one social class, one vocation, or one ethnicity, nor do they all possess the same level of education or have the same gifts and ministry. Rather, what all the saints share is that they were receptive to the grace of God in their life, and, thankfully, they did not get in the way of God's work in them. By allowing God to love them to the full, hundreds, thousands, and even millions of people reaped the fruits of the grace of God through their receptivity. If we really want to imitate the saints and become holy, then like them, we must not resist God's grace and therefore become an obstacle to God's plan of salvation. Rather, we must welcome the grace of God in our lives in every moment, because by doing so we will be welcoming our own salvation and the salvation of others.

26
Who Is God?

"Being in an agony he prayed more earnestly; and his sweat became like great drops of blood falling down upon the ground."
—Luke 22:42–44

When I was a teenager, my father worked third shift. As I was preparing to go to sleep at night, my father would be preparing to leave the house and go to work. When I would wake up in the morning refreshed and ready to begin a new day, my father was coming home from work exhausted and ready to go to sleep. It happened often that during baseball practice in the evening I would be out on the field and occasionally look over in the stands and see my dad's head nodding as he was struggling to stay awake. Sometimes he would give up the struggle altogether and stretch out on the grass to take a nap. Occasionally, I remember thinking as I saw my father sleeping and the other parents clapping and cheering for their son, *Doesn't my dad care about me? Doesn't he want to watch me?* This would leave me at times sad and angry, because when I saw my father sleeping in the stands, this did not appear to be what I thought love was or should look like.

Many years later as I would grow up and mature, I realized that my dad's falling asleep at my baseball games was exactly what love looked like. Why? Because it was love that was poured out, stretched beyond its limits. My father fell asleep during my baseball practice as he was giving his whole self to me and our family. If my father could have chosen any hours to work, he would have, like most people, worked during the day. Unfortunately, he did not have that choice; however, one thing he did choose was to embrace this cross for me and our family. The weight of this cross was revealed by his falling asleep during my baseball practice.

To arrive at this understanding, I needed to open my eyes more and readjust my heart so that I could perceive and understand more deeply the truth of what was occurring. Like all of us, I had an image and an idea of what love is and what I thought it should look like, especially in my life. The truth was that my image and idea of love was self-centered and therefore narrow and inadequate. A very similar thing can be said about us with God. We need to readjust not only our eyes but also our hearts, because very often our ideas and images of God are too small.

Over the years, I have projected onto God many silly and immature thoughts. I have often wondered, *Does God see me? Does God care about me? Why does he not give me what I want and what I think I need? Why does he let one person succeed and another person fail?* These are all normal human questions. However, what they all have in common is that they are attempting to remove God's divinity and fill it with our humanity, limiting God to our human way of seeing, judging, and evaluating. In other words, these thoughts are attempting to make God like us. For many people, "God" is nothing else but an exalted image of themselves, a sort of superhuman version of oneself.

In St. Paul's letter to the Philippians, he says that Jesus *"emptied himself, taking the form of a servant, being born in the likeness of men."* As if those words were not both profound and puzzling enough, St. Paul continues speaking about Jesus and says that *"Being found in human form he humbled himself and became obedient unto death, even death on a cross" (Philippians 2:7–8).*

Can these mysterious words by St. Paul be true? Perhaps he is exaggerating a bit or being too emotional. Maybe St. Paul is attempting to speak here about Jesus more as a poet than as a theologian. Nonetheless, we must ask ourselves, has God really emptied himself and become a slave? The Gospels confirm this remarkable truth. In the Agony in the Garden we are told that Jesus *"withdrew from them . . . and knelt down and prayed, 'Father, if you are willing, remove this chalice from me; nevertheless not my will, but yours, be done.' . . . And being in an agony he prayed more earnestly; and his sweat became like great drops of blood falling down upon the ground" (Luke 22:41–44).*

St. Paul is right! God in Jesus has become a servant, who for our sake became obedient to death on a cross. What these aspects reveal to us about God is not only his great love and humility, but also his vulnerability. Being vulnerable is described as being capable of being physically wounded and open to attack or damage. Various synonyms for *vulnerable* include weak, defenseless, helpless, and exposed. This is who God is and who he allows himself to be for our sake. We can see this throughout Jesus's entire life, but we witness it most profoundly in his Passion.

For example, Jesus was weak and needed Simon of Cyrene to help him carry his cross *(Luke 23:26)*. Before Pilate, Jesus was defenseless and kept silent, making no attempt to defend himself *(Mark 15:2–5)*. Jesus was helpless, with nobody to come to his aid physically *(Mark 15:17–20)*. Jesus was exposed. He died naked on a cross like a criminal and with criminals *(Luke 23:32–33)*.

Is it not true then to speak about God as being vulnerable? If it is, then where is this angry God that some people speak about? Where is this God who only likes certain people and hates others that some talk about? Where is this self-serving God who is checked out from our lives, that some people speak of? The answer is that *that* God doesn't exist, and Jesus Christ is the proof of that!

If this is the way God is with us, it is important to ask ourselves, *What are we like before God? Are we vulnerable before him? Or do we attempt to be independent, self-sufficient, and closed off from his grace?* Despite what others may say and even what we may feel and think at times, it is impossible for God to be absent or distant from our lives. *"If I ascend to heaven,"* the Psalmist writes, *"you are there! If I make my bed in Sheol, you are there! If I take the wings of the morning and dwell in the uttermost parts of the sea, even there your hand shall lead me, and your right hand shall hold me" (Psalm*

139:8–10). Therefore, if there is anyone who is absent or distant in our relationship with God, it is us!

Personally, I have realized that when I am self-absorbed, preoccupied, and anxious with many things, God appears the most distant to me. Hence, when I am not engaging God personally in my life, being vulnerable before him, he appears distant.

This is important to consider because of the temptation, which I believe all of us face at times, to believe that holiness or at the very least a healthy spiritual life will consist of great experiences of God, tremendous theological insights, or even the affirmation and recognition of others. Surely our relationship with God will include all those things to some degree; however, the real measure of a healthy spiritual life is when a person is attempting to imitate Christ in his vulnerability. When a person who, like Christ, makes themselves vulnerable and therefore available both to God and others, they are on the path of genuine spiritual growth. True holiness then is dependent on our level of vulnerability.

St. Teresa of Calcutta spent forty years with minimal sensible experience or consolation from God. As strange as this might appear to some, this is in fact quite normal in the spiritual life. The more we advance in holiness, the less God communicates to us through our senses, because the more we grow in holiness, the more God communicates to us directly through our spirit, which is often not a sensible experience. St. John of the Cross explains it this way:

> The reason for this dryness is that God transfers his goods and strength from sense to spirit. Since the sensory part of the soul is incapable of the goods of the spirit, it remains deprived, dry, and empty. Thus, while the spirit is tasting, the flesh tastes nothing at all and becomes weak in its work. But through this nourishment the spirit grows stronger and more alert, and becomes more solicitous than before about not failing God.[32]

St. Teresa spent forty years of her life, from a purely human perspective, in the dark. This means that God was not appearing to her, whether in person or through some sensory experience, and telling her each moment of the day what to do and say and how to act in every situation. Nor did God appear to her at the end of each day to explain to her everything that had happened so she could understand things better.

Some people mistakenly have the notion that a saint is someone who lives in constant sensible communion with God or one who is continually having extraordinary experiences of God. For most of the saints this is not true, so why would it be for us? A saint is a person who lives in deep communion with God, but it is a communion through faith, since, as St. Paul reminds us, *"we walk by faith, not by sight" (2 Corinthians 5:7)*. St. Teresa is a saint, and this is true of all the saints, not because of her experiences of God, but because her entire life was rooted in faith, and it was this faith that opened her heart so deeply to the mysterious and often confusing ways of God. Hence, it was her deep faith that enabled her to be vulnerable before God and therefore led her to the heights of holiness.

In our relationship with God, have we, like Jesus, emptied ourselves and taken the form of a slave? Have we become obedient to the cross in our life and allowed it to form us, or are we simply holding on to ourselves for ourselves? The greatest problem in my life is that I haven't emptied myself enough and haven't imitated Jesus by becoming a servant. Nor have I always embraced the crosses in my life and allowed them to form me and teach me. Therefore, I am not always vulnerable before God, and as a result I struggle, doubt, and do not trust God completely, simply because there is too much of me in the way. If we wish to become holy like St. Teresa and all the saints, and if we wish to follow the example of Jesus, we must imitate them in their vulnerability before God, because by doing so we make ourselves totally available to him and therefore allow him to do with us as he desires.

27
Be Who You Are in God

"Let your light so shine before men, that they may see your good works and give glory to your Father who is in heaven."
—Matthew 5:16

A good friend of mine who is a Benedictine monk recently told me a story about a man who attends Mass every Sunday at his monastery. This man—we will call him Steven—lives several miles from the monastery, and every morning while he is on his way to work, Steven deliberately drives twenty minutes out of his way just so he can drive past the monastery. He doesn't have time to join the monks for prayer or even to stop for a minute or two to savor the silence and stillness of the grounds. All he can do is drive past the monastery, and this, as strange as it may appear, is enough for him. When my friend asked Steven why he did this he responded with utter frankness and sincerity: "Father, most of my day I witness people lying, cheating, gossiping, and slandering one another. When I drive past the monastery every morning I am reminded of the purpose of my life and how God desires me to live. Though I am weak and fall into some of these things myself, my drive past the monastery each morning strengthens my resolve to live a holy life."

What I found peculiar and so interesting about his motivation for driving past the monastery is that it had nothing to do with the monks personally. Steven did not have a particular friendship with any of these monks. He wasn't attracted to their preaching, and none of the monks, so far as he knew, had gifts such as healing, prophecy, or reading hearts that tend to attract people. Rather, these monks led a simple and quiet life of prayer and work and did absolutely nothing to promote themselves individually or as a community. There wasn't then anything externally unique or sentimental regarding the monks that would lead Steven to drive twenty minutes out of his way each morning on his way to work. The monks, to their credit and much to their surprise if they knew this, were just being who they were called to be in God. By doing so, they were for this man and for many others *"the salt of the earth"* and *"the light of the world" (Matthew 5:13–14).*

In the Gospel of Matthew, shortly after the Beatitudes Jesus gives us this call to be salt and light to others. The Beatitudes, as we reflected on earlier in this book, are the genuine path of transformation for every disciple of Christ. Therefore, they are the genuine path of true happiness for each one of us. This happiness that only God can give us is not meant to be kept merely for ourselves. Rather, we must share it with others. Hence, through Jesus's call to be *"the salt of the earth"* and *"the light of the world"* he is reminding us that holiness is never merely a private endeavor.

Of course, each one of us has a personal relationship with God. We all have a personal prayer life that is sustained and nourished by times of solitude. However, all these things that are essential for our relationship with God are not meant only for us. Jesus reiterates this point when he tells us, *"Let your light so shine before men, that they may see your good works and give glory to your Father who is in heaven" (Matthew 5:16).* Despite what some Christians may say or how they might choose to live, there is no such thing as a "me and Jesus" spirituality. Whether we live in a monastery or in the world, whether we are old or young, and whether we have studied theology or not, Jesus is reminding us that the Christian life is meant to be shared. St. John Chrysostom elaborates on this when he writes, *"The person characterized by humility, gentleness, mercy and righteousness does not build a fence around good deeds. Rather, that one ensures that these good fountains overflow for the benefit of others."*[33]

The question then remains, *With whom are we meant to share our Christian life?* Jesus tells the disciples at the end of the Gospel of Matthew to *"Go therefore and make disciples of all nations . . . teaching them to observe all that I have commanded you" (Matthew 28:19–20)*, and St. Peter instructs us to *"Always be prepared to make a defense to anyone who calls you to account for the hope that is in you" (1 Peter 3:15)*. As disciples of Jesus, we must be ready to proclaim the gospel with our lips and our words whenever and to whomever the Lord calls us to do so. However, for most people most of the time, the best way to share the gospel is by being who we really are in God with whomever we are sharing life in the present moment.

The distinctive characteristic of salt is that it preserves something from going bad, whereas the distinctive characteristic of light is that it illuminates. How do we preserve something from going bad, and how do we illuminate something, namely the presence of Jesus Christ in our lives? The answer is very simple; it's by being who we are in God. The last part, "in God," is necessary, because without it we leave out the one who is most important: Jesus. Without Jesus we will most certainly not preserve or illuminate anything.

I once met a very devout Christian who owned a hardware store. During our conversation he expressed to me that his chief desire in life was to live the gospel as authentically as he could. When I asked him how specifically he did that he told me that each morning he prayed for the grace to see his employees, customers, and everyone else he would meet that day as Jesus and therefore treat them accordingly. He viewed his business not primarily as a means of financial gain, but as an opportunity to evangelize and share the love of Jesus with others. This man's priority was not to be a successful businessman, but rather to be who he truly was in God.

Regardless of our profession in this world, we can apply this man's same principle to our life. If I am a doctor, it would be well worth considering each day, *How would Jesus treat my patients? How would he speak with them?* If I am a parent, it could be helpful to prayerfully consider, *How is Jesus inviting me today to love my children? How or what does he want me to say to them today?* If I am a priest I must ask Jesus, *How does he want me to proclaim the gospel to my congregation both when I am preaching at church or when I am involved in some administrative task? How can I bring the love of Jesus to those in my congregation who are sick or lonely, or who feel left out?* Seeing our profession in life, whatever it may be, as a means for spreading the gospel not only enables us to become more authentic disciples but also protects us from turning the Christian faith into a job that we do for a period of time each day or each week. With God's grace over time this attitude allows our faith to grow and mature, and in turn we become the people we are meant to be in God.

Often, people will give the following advice to someone about life: "Just be yourself, and everything will work out fine." For the most part I believe this advice is very well intended; however, when I hear it, my body becomes tense, and despite all my best efforts a worried and concerned look always appears very quickly on my face. The reason I have this reaction is that if a person is not living in God, or is not attempting to live in God, then the self you are being and consequently transmitting to others is not your best self. In other words, if God is absent from a person's life it will be impossible for them to be "*the salt of the earth*" and "*the light of the world,*" because the Beatitudes are not present in this person's life. Who then are you being? Your natural self might not be bad, but without God there is very little good that one can do, and therefore there will be very little transformation experienced by anyone.

St. Paul says to the Corinthians that when he came to them he appeared "*in weakness and in much fear and trembling; and my speech and my message were not in plausible words of wisdom" (1 Corinthians 2:3–4)*. Even though this may appear to the Corinthians as an obstacle to being salt and light, St. Paul testifies that his message to them, namely the preaching of the gospel, is "*in demonstration of the Spirit and of power, (so) that your faith might not rest in the wisdom of men but in the power of God" (1 Corinthians 1:2:4–5).* St. Paul did not put on a mask or adopt some foreign personality to try and convert the Corinthians. Nor did he try to hide or deny his own human weaknesses. Rather, he came to them as he was. On the surface, as St. Paul said, he was weak, fearful, and not the best public speaker. However, his proclamation of the gospel was effective because despite his human weaknesses, he was living the Beatitudes, and therefore he was able to be salt and light to others.

Throughout the history of Christianity, the various churches, ministries, and religious orders have always considered how they can increase their numbers. After all, we want as many people as possible to know the good news of the gospel. To reach more people, Christians throughout history have prayerfully discerned many creative and effective ways to proclaim the gospel, whether that involved things like street evangelization, the use of technology, or greater outreach to the poor, unbelievers, and the sick, etc. All of this obviously is good and necessary. However, the more each one of us is attempting to be who we really are in God, the greater fruit our evangelization and ministries will experience. St. Catherine of Siena, who knew this reality well, once said, *"Be who you were created to be, and you will set the world on fire."*[34] There is then no great secret to holiness and evangelization; it occurs most naturally when we are being who we really are in God. If we strive for that, then we may find we won't have to work so hard at everything else.

Notes

1 *Vatican Council II. Volume 1. Decree on the Ministry and Life of Priests* (Costello Publishing Company, 2004), 868–69.
2 James V. Schall, S.J., "*The Reason for the Seasons: Why Christians Celebrate What and When They Do*" (Sophia Institute Press, 2018), 113.
3 *The Collected Works of St. John of the Cross: The Spiritual Canticle* (Institute of Carmelite Studies, 1991), 482.
4 *The Collected Works of St. John of the Cross: The Letters* (Institute of Carmelite Studies, 1991), 760.
5 *The Sayings of the Desert Fathers* (Cistercian Publications, 1975), 28–29.
6 Thomas Merton, *New Seeds of Contemplation* (New Directions, 2007), 34.
7 Lawrence Cunningham, *Francis of Assisi: Performing the Gospel of Life* (Eerdmans, 2004), 9.
8 Pope Benedict XVI, *Doctors of the Church, Our Sunday Visitor,* 2011.
9 *An Ancient Christian Commentary on Scripture, Matthew 1-13* (InterVarsity Press, 2001), 55–56.
10 *The Encyclicals of Benedict XVI* (Catholic Truth Society, 2013), 7.
11 *The Collected Works of St. John of the Cross: The Spiritual Canticle,* 479.
12 G. K. Chesterton; *St. Francis of Assisi* (Hendrickson Pub., 2008), n.p.
13 *Catechism of the Catholic Church,* 1718.
14 *An Ancient Christian Commentary on Scripture, Matthew 1-13,* 80.
15 *The Collected Works of St. John of the Cross: The Ascent of Mount Carmel,* Book Two, Chapter 13 (Institute of Carmelite Studies, 1991), 190.

16 *The Collected Works of St. John of the Cross: The Ascent of Mount Carmel*, Book Two, Chapter 13, 190.

17 *The Complete Mystical Works of Meister Eckhart*, trans. Bernard McGinn (Crossroad Publishing Company, 2009), 96.

18 Jean-Pierre de Caussade, *Abandonment to Divine Providence*, (Doubleday, 1975), 23.

19 *The Westminster Collection of Christian Quotations*, compiled by Martin H. Manser (Westminster John Knox Press, 2001), 92.

20 Scott Hahn, *Catholic Bible Dictionary* (Doubleday, 2009), 802–803.

21 https://research.lifeway.com/2022/01/28/1-in-7-global-christians-faced-persecution-in-2021/. Accessed 13 December 2024.

22 John Paul II, *Rosarium Virginis Mariae*, #9.

23 *The Collected Works of St. John of the Cross: The Living Flame of Love* (Institute of Carmelite Studies, 1991), 686.

24 Frances Kelly Nemeck, O.M.I., and Marie Theresa Coombs, Hermit, *Contemplation* (Wipf and Stock, 2001), 15.

25 Nemeck and Coombs, *Contemplation*, 16.

26 *Vatican Council II. Volume 1. Dogmatic Constitution on the Church* (Costello Publishing Company, 2004), 396–97.

27 Jean-Pierre de Caussade, *Abandonment to Divine Providence*, 24.

28 Peter Kreeft, *How to be Holy: First steps in Becoming a Saint* (Ignatius Press, 2016), 17.

29 *Catechism of the Catholic Church*, 904.

30 *Catechism of the Catholic Church*, 508–509.

31 *The Philokalia, Volume 1: On Guarding the Intellect: Twenty-seven texts*, St. Isaiah the Solitary (Faber and Faber, 1979), 24.

32 *The Collected Works of St. John of the Cross: The Dark Night* (Institute of Carmelite Studies, 1991), 378.

33 *An Ancient Christian Commentary on Scripture, Matthew 1-13*, 93.

34 Gulnaaz Saif, *Passion to Profession* (Walnut Publication, 2020), 8.

ABOUT PARACLETE PRESS

PARACLETE PRESS IS THE PUBLISHING ARM of the Cape Cod Benedictine community, the Community of Jesus. Presenting a full expression of Christian belief and practice, we reflect the ecumenical charism of the Community and its dedication to sacred music, the fine arts, and the written word.

Learn more about us at our website:
www.paracletepress.com
or phone us toll-free at 1.800.451.5006

SCAN
TO
READ
MORE

YOU MAY ALSO ENJOY